COMPUTERS, SCHOOLS AND STUDENTS

Monitoring Change in Education

Series Editor:
J. Mark Halstead
University of Huddersfield, UK

Change is a key characteristic of the worlds of business, education and industry and the rapidity of change underlines an urgent need to analyze, evaluate and, where appropriate, correct its direction. The series is aimed at contributing to this analysis. Its unique contribution consists of making sense of changes in education and in offering a timely and considered response to new challenges; the series, therefore, focuses on contemporary issues and does so with academic rigour.

Other titles in the series

Globalisation, Education and Culture Shock
Edited by
Cedric Cullingford and Stan Gunn
ISBN 978 0 7546 4201 5

Risk, Education and Culture
Edited by
Andrew Hope and Paul Oliver
ISBN 978 0 7546 4172 8

Race and Ethnicity in Education
Ranjit Arora
ISBN 978 0 7546 1441 8

Mentoring in Education
An International Perspective
Edited by
Cedric Cullingford
ISBN 978 0 7546 4577 1

Young Disabled People
Aspirations, Choices and Constraints
Sonali Shah
ISBN 978 0 7546 7422 1

Computers, Schools and Students
The Effects of Technology

CEDRIC CULLINGFORD and NUSRAT HAQ
University of Huddersfield, UK

ASHGATE

Published by
Ashgate Publishing Limited
Wey Court East
Union Road
Farnham
Surrey, GU9 7PT
England

Ashgate Publishing Company
Suite 420
101 Cherry Street
Burlington
VT 05401-4405
USA

www.ashgate.com

British Library Cataloguing in Publication Data
Cullingford, Cedric.
    Computers, schools and students : the effects of
    technology.-- (Monitoring change in education)
    1. Education, Secondary--Great Britain--Data processing
    2. Computer-assisted instruction--Great Britain--
    Evaluation. 3. Computers and children.
    I. Title II. Series III. Haq, Nusrat.
    373.1'334'0941-dc22

Library of Congress Cataloging-in-Publication Data
Cullingford, Cedric.
    Computers, schools, and students: the effects of technology / by Cedric Cullingford and Nusrat Haq.
       p. cm. -- (Monitoring change in education)
    Includes index.
    ISBN 978-0-7546-7821-2 (hardback) -- ISBN 978-0-7546-9613-1 (ebook)
    1. Information technology--Study and teaching (Secondary)--Great Britain. 2. Education, Secondary--Great Britain. I. Haq, Nusrat. II. Title.

    T58.5.C83 2009
    373.133'40941--dc22

2009007640

ISBN   978-0-7546-7821-2
EISBN 978-0-7546-9613-1

Mixed Sources
Product group from well-managed
forests and other controlled sources
www.fsc.org Cert no. SGS-COC-2482
© 1996 Forest Stewardship Council

Printed and bound in Great Britain by
TJ International Ltd, Padstow, Cornwall

Contents

For Nusrat's Father and in memory of her Mother

Preface

The effects and implications of computers are not always fully understood. This is understandable since on one level they are ubiquitous and taken for granted so that it is difficult to measure how they affect the ways in which people think. While there have been many new technologies introduced over time, with ever increasing rapidity, nothing has made as far reaching an impact as information technology.

Computers are changing the modes of transaction between people. This is a global phenomenon. There are fewer boundaries of time and space. Communication is instant. This has a marked influence on the way business is carried out, not only in terms of financial transactions in which millions in notional value can be wiped out in an instant, but also in terms of the ways in which people go about their daily lives, with online shopping, betting, auctions, payments and many other transactions.

Computers change modes of communication but also access to information. It is not only publishing that is changing, but also how people think about knowledge. There is very little that is hard to access, even if the quality of what is offered is very mixed. Part of this plethora of information is presented as entertainment, and computers add their special extra of interactivity.

The structural changes to the means of communication are clear. What is less clear are the effects on people's patterns of thought and behaviour. Does such ubiquitous communication affect the ways in which people understand each other? Does the medium have an effect on democracy or on prejudice? How profound are the results of the technology? Are people's lives so much changed?

If McLuhan, writing 40 years ago, is still invoked, it is because of his excited belief that the medium is the message, and the implication that has been continued and reiterated that the effects of computing must be profound. The sense of impending change and huge potential has been demonstrated in the educational world. That spirit of optimism and speculation continues unabated.

This book, however, is about empirical evidence. It is not about the possibilities presented by computer programs, but about the reality of school. It presents evidence about the ways students experience computers in school, their attitudes towards them and how they use them. The context of their home life is of significance, but the concentration is on the daily rituals of the school.

There are two levels that emerge from the analysis. There remains the fascination with the new, with the possibilities and the potential. There has been much research on different programs and on concept mapping, and millions of pounds, euros and dollars have been spent on research on these subjects. And then there is what takes place in schools, on which there has been far less research and even fewer grants for research.

Students find themselves in an odd position. They are nowadays familiar with computers, and use them easily every day, just as they are surrounded by all the other applications of the technology from mobile phones to i-pods. We need to understand how they are coping with ICT in schools. Are their knowledge and experience seriously enhanced? How do schools cope with all the demands made on them? How do they use the new technology to its best advantage?

This book is a journey through the processes of thought both about computers and about schools. The evidence comes from the students but it is, as a result, sympathetic to the teachers who have to cope with a huge new challenge. The question to be explored is whether schools are able or equipped to meet this challenge and whether they have the support they deserve.

Chapter 1

The Introduction of Information Technology

Change can make some people feel bewildered. For others change is fascinating because it is full of possibilities. While people have always been aware of continuing changes in society in terms of attitudes, power, control and morality, there used to be a debate about whether change was a good or a bad thing. We now live in a time in which change is supposed to be inevitable and therefore is not to be doubted. The questions are no longer about its utility, its threats or beneficence, but about how to adapt to it.

This sense of inevitability stems from the fact that change is associated essentially with technology. Change is nowadays not a question of historical or human progress, but of new systems of communication and production. For many years people debated the effects of new technological inventions like the steam engine and the steam presses that allowed the manufacture of millions of books, magazines and newspapers, very quickly and at unprecedented low cost. The implications of mass manufacture for people's lives have been profound. However, the greatest attention has been paid to the inventions themselves, rather than their consequences.

Like all modern technologies, computers are fascinating in themselves, in their rapid development and increasing applications. The effects on people are less well understood. While we might have learned something about human nature from the horrors of the twentieth century with its world wars and the Holocaust, we know for certain that the wars gave rise to rapid advances in technological invention.

One such invention to which the horrors of war gave such a boost was the computer. While the original idea can be traced to Babbitt, the impetus for its development is more associated with Bletchley Park. The demonstration of the power of technology soon led to a belief in its transforming abilities.

The belief that the world "will" be transformed by information technology goes back a long way and has been couched in the same visionary language for 50 years. While McLuhan (1967) asserted the power of the means of communication over the processes of thought, the belief in transformation specifically through computers was applied in particular to systems of education. The claim was twofold: that systems of communication would change the way people think, and that they would transform schools. Evans (1981) thought that the microelectronic revolution would bring an end to war, poverty, crime and ignorance. Franklin (1990) typically likened technology to democracy: "Like democracy, technology changes the social and individual relationships between us. It has forced us to examine and redefine our notion of power and of accountability" (p. 12).

It is, however, the transformation of education that has led to the most powerful assertions. Westly (1989) described computer technology as the atomic bomb of the information age that would break the barrier between learning and entertainment. There have been many statements supporting the notion that, by themselves, by their sheer existence, computers will change the world (Department of Education and Science 1981, Papert 1993). There are many examples of the same sentiment: "Educational computer usage could change the face of education in a very short space of time" (Underwood 1994). Usually any doubt that would be expressed by the word "could" is excluded by "will":

> The next generation of students will be increasingly empowered and aware consumers, with a wide choice of educational products (Society for Research into Higher Education. (1996, p. 34)

> Our children will be leaving school IT literate, having been able to exploit the best that technology can offer. (National Grid for Learning 1997, p. 3)

The National Grid for Learning is a good example of a belief that the availability of information technology will have a profound effect on schools. Those who are aware of what can be done with technology and who marvel at its potential see the effects on schools as (eventually) inevitable and profound.

> ICT challenges current descriptions and practice of pedagogy, in terms of all prescriptions of time, place, authority and the purpose of teaching. (Loveless 2002, p. 4)

The ubiquity of the technology is clear, not only its availability in schools, but also in its permeation of everyday life. The question remains of what impact it is having on schools and on the education of children.

Great belief and massive investment have been made in technology before. It is no coincidence that the development of the state education system took place at the same time as the rise of the mass reading public, another result of technology. The application of steam presses to printing made the production of cheap texts possible for the first time, which were seized on by those who realized the opportunity they gave for instruction and at the same time devoured by those who sought entertainment (Altick 1957). The greater availability of books, pamphlets and newspapers, as well as tracts and chapbooks, and the profusion of outlets like WH Smith were the first great signs of the impact of new communication systems (McLuhan 1962).

There were many people in the early nineteenth century who believed in the transforming power of the new technology. Access to great works of literature, let alone the Bible, was seen as a huge educational opportunity. There was a strong belief that access to great literature through the development of reading, and the exploitation of this ability by the promotion of sermons, tracts and other religious literature, would transform the spiritual and moral life of the nation. Reading had previously been confined to a minority, not only because of the lack of educational opportunities but also because printed material, and not only leatherbound books, was so expensive and therefore restricted. The chances that were offered to transform the lives of the masses, especially at a time of major technological development that was radically changing the working and domestic lives of the population, were eagerly seized upon in faith and hope.

In the event, and despite all the endeavour, the results were disappointing. Although the opportunities were taken up by some, giving rise to a quite new conception of literacy (Hoggart 1957), the results of mass reading were somewhat disconcerting. Instead of making use of the opportunity to read Shakespeare, the Bible and all the religious tracts, the reading public sought far easier entertainment. They relished the use of literacy for light relief rather than instruction. The technological changes in the spread of printed materials brought about a mass reading public with mass tastes, seeking sensation and easily acquired entertainment rather than elevating texts. Dickens gives telling accounts of the ways in which religious material was used (for example, to light a pipe) and read (for example, focusing on sensational horrors from which people had to be saved, ignoring the subsequent conversion and the preaching that went with them).

New technologies since then have been presented as opportunities for both greater pleasure and education. The introduction of radio, for example, was seen as part of the break-down of barriers of understanding through greater communication. This meant that it could inform as well as entertain, although radio was first used as a public medium for leisure as much as for the "broadcasting" of information.

When the radio was first introduced, it was seen as being of great potential in education and in the 1920s educational radio was presented to schools and still used as a huge technological advantage for teachers (Plomp and Ely 1996). The broadcasting of educational programs was seen as an opportunity for pupils to have access to knowledge that was more entertaining as well as more instructive.

If radio was seized on as an aid to schools, the introduction of television presented an even greater opportunity. Symbolized by distance learning operations like the Open University, which delivered its materials through public service broadcasting stations, television was presented as the ultimate educational aid (Schramm 1997). The best instructors supported by clear diagrams, visual material and moving pictures rather than still ones – this was seen as a means not just of enhancing teachers but also of replacing them.

Instructional radio and television were seized upon as the best resourced and most appealing forms of programmed learning. Technology was to come to the aid of learning in a way that was assumed to be irresistible. As we now know, however, the impact of television has been almost wholly on leisure. While a great deal is learned through the medium, this is inadvertent rather than a deliberate activity. Whilst it can be argued that television superseded the radio, and was in turn usurped by the computer, there was, in fact, no time when the medium of communication in itself was anything more than a peripheral extra. None of the media ever became central to instruction. Attempts all over the world to enhance lessons by additional resources have been undermined not so much by lack of resources as by the dictates of the curriculum, by the text books, the tests and the desire to make sure that teachers know exactly what students have learned (Alexander 2000).

Nevertheless, the belief in educational technology was strong in the 1960s and the 1970s. The National Council for Educational Technology was founded in 1969 following reports of the Committee on Audiovisual Aids. The Association for Programmed Learning added "Educational Technology" to its title in 1968, and the United States created a National Centre of Educational Technology in 1970. There are many examples and a number of histories of the rise of educational resource centres in schools and attempts to centre the whole of the school, and its ethos, around them. Such enterprise seems quite dated now.

One of the reasons for the lack of penetration of these earlier forms of educational technology, unlike books, is the fact that they are passive media. They are like a teacher to the extent that the listener simply receives ideas without response. They are unlike teachers insofar as they cannot allow iterative dialogue. The early theories of instructional technology saw them as an aid, an extra, alongside the teacher, the textbook and the blackboard. It was soon realized that the best means of learning were not simply through delivering a curriculum, but through two-way communication. What was sought from educational technology was the ideal of interactivity (Garrison 1993). The ideal learning environment is a dialogue between teachers and students and amongst students themselves. One of the reasons for the displacement of one technology by another is the desire to provide the receiver with more to do than simply watch and listen. Educational technology is another reminder of the difference between the ideal conditions of learning, and the policy of detailed and controlled teaching.

While each new medium has been hailed as a significant breakthrough on its introduction, there is something different about the potential of computers. Educational technology was first envisaged as an extension of programmed learning, which, based on behaviourist principles, did at least suggest reactions by the pupils. More entertaining media cannot insist on more than a passive response. Such passivity is what the mass audience prefers rather than more demanding and cerebral attention (Cullingford 1984). Creating the conditions by which viewers will be guaranteed to pay close attention is difficult (Sturm 1991).

The tensions between the uses of instruction and the pleasures of entertainment will always be there. Each medium is dominated by the programs that are the most popular or the easiest to watch or play around with. There has always been a reaction against those forms of communication that are most demanding. This remains true of all the latest communication media, like i-pods. New systems create different habits of banking and transferring goods, but they also transform habits of entertainment. The computer itself is symbolic of that dual role.

Nevertheless, the excitement and the hope surrounding the introduction of information and communications technology (ICT) has been based on the possibilities of what each individual can do with it. As in the ideal of programmed learning, the computer does not merely present material but can be adjusted to react. The potential for interaction suggests that computer technology is different. While any medium can be controlled in terms of pace and timing, there is not the same scope for multiple interactions. Online interactions are believed to result in higher learning outcomes in students. Overhead projectors send out pictures. A calculator will respond to different instructions in handling numeric information. A computer has the capacity to be a huge and dynamic library.

The potential for storage, and access to, a vast amount of information makes the computer different, but more important still could be the way information can be manipulated. The control lies in the hands of the operator. It is because of this that the development of the microprocessor is so important. Computers have changed our lives and microprocessors have changed computers.

The way computers have been introduced into schools has been slow and piecemeal. This is partly as a result of the constant changes in the capacity of the programs and power of storage. There is no moment of stasis. In 1957 there was a conference that attempted to introduce computing techniques into the school setting (Barker 1971). In the 1960s, some schools introduced elements of computing into mathematics, coinciding with a general sense that the United Kingdom was falling behind in computer technology. It was in the 1970s that tutorial software was first developed and used initially in universities. The Microelectronic Education program was set up in 1981 to help schools prepare children to use microelectronics and to help teachers learn how to teach it (Wellington 1985). This was the time when most schools acquired computers and started teaching courses in information technology.

Information technology was seen as a combination of computing, microelectronics and telecommunications. The Microelectronic Education program promoted curriculum development, teacher education, resource organization and support. The most recent attempt to make a radical difference to the use and availability of computers in schools was the National Grid for Learning, promising all schools better connection to the numerous resources of the international information "superhighway". Promises were made about teacher education and guarantees given that pupils would be computer literate. Each new initiative is a suggestion that, despite the earlier beliefs and investment, there has not been a major breakthrough in the performance of schools despite all their best efforts. The energy and passion are considerable, and yet the results disappointing.

The sense of disappointment does not come about because the technology is not being used. On the contrary, technology pervades every part of people's lives, from automatic teller machines to online shopping. More insistently, the communication systems of e-mail and mobile phones demonstrate the ubiquity of people's changing patterns of living. The disappointment lies in the fact that there are dichotomies between the use of computers for entertainment, like games and music, and their utility for education. Despite the many programs that have been developed, and the insistence that all teaching awards are linked to using ICT, and despite the curiosity shown in measuring the effects of different computer uses, there is always a sense, boosted by so many statements by the Departments of Education, that more needs to be done.

The policy makers insist on the importance of ICT. The problem is that there have been few coherent reasons to support this, as opposed to general expectations. The reasons for the introduction of ICT into schools have varied over the years. The major motives for the use of ICT education can also be to some extent contradictory.

There are several reasons for the teaching of ICT (Hawkridge 1991):

- Computers are important in society and students should therefore learn to live with them.
- Computers can improve teaching in all areas of the curriculum.
- Computers will create changes in the nature of learning and alter the educational system.
- Computers will improve the country's economuy through hardware and software capacity.
- Computers will replace teachers.

From the point of view of schools, these are very different issues to deal with. While schools are always engaged in attempting to reconcile conflicting demands – individual expression, social coherence and academic excellence, all of which need to be treated differently (Egan 1997) – the fact that computers have so many different significances creates a whole new problem, like the central one of whether computing should be taught as a skill or as an aid in support of the main curriculum.

Every time that the government cajoles schools into doing more in the way of ICT, it puts extra pressure on them. The commands might be well meant, but they are not well thought through. Exactly how are schools to deal with ICT? Apart from the difficulty of trying to keep up with new computer technology, schools face pressures of different kinds. Along with political pressure come demands for higher quality and to meet employment requirements, together with industrial innovations and social experimentation and commercial opportunities. Then there are the expectations and hopes of parents (Underwood and Underwood 1990).

Equipping a pupil for the demands of industry and with social awareness of communication systems are not the same thing. Political pressure is the question of control. Many people have pointed out that ICT gives a means of greater control and greater centralization. One can control access to knowledge (Hennessey 1993).

> What should be automated, or rather, who should decide? It is not a question about technology, but about political power. a recognition of the degree to which social antagonisms are mediated by technology. (Beynon 1992, p. 13)

When the government chides schools for not doing enough and teachers for not being up-to-date, this is because it is concerned with the skills of a potential income-generating work force, not the excitement of learning through access to information. Computers are claimed by some to enable educational provision to be more effective and by others to make it more efficient. There are many tensions between these conflicting demands and, in the overriding belief in technology, these conflicts are rarely explored.

Schools are not in an easy position. The expectations vary, but they remain strong. The assumption that computers are a wholly good thing has not helped people study the implications for schools. The widespread belief that one day ICT will transform all learning by individualizing it has not come about. There are still some doubts about what is really happening in schools. Some suggest that we are still in the 'dark ages', and far from seeing the light. There are many pessimistic analyses of the impact of technology on schools (Cuban 1986). Others question whether children's use of computers can be automatically equated with their using them in a creative way. And then, together with a realization that computers are mostly used for entertainment, and that the younger generations are far more skilled in their use, there is the knowledge that new technology gives access to a whole range of minority interests from pornography to gambling, from manuals on how to make bombs to Internet dating and chat rooms.

The more the subject is studied, the more complex it becomes. It is not simply a matter of asserting that ICT is a good thing and will transform schools. ICT transforms access to information and transforms communication. It does not necessarily transform people.

Conclusions

Information technology has an obvious impact, but it is not a simple one. We can learn from the ways in which earlier technologies were introduced, from printed material to television. A shared belief as well as hope that the technology will have a beneficial and transforming effect is undermined by the reality that the technology is used not so much as an educational tool as a means of entertainment and mass communication.

There have been many attempts to introduce the new technology into the education system, but the results have generally been disappointing, partly because the school system has hardly changed for decades. There is a clash between the ethos of schools and the ways in which ICT operates, and the effects of the new media have not been thought through by policy makers. Schools find themselves under external pressure, strong but incoherent.

Chapter 2
The Relationship between Computers and Schools

Like other organizations, schools inevitably have to come to terms with the new modes of communication, and with the new machines that deal with matters like the recording of results and finance. There is a natural pressure on schools to adapt to the new technology, the same impulse that drives teachers, like anyone else, to use computers in their everyday lives. At the same time, it is abundantly clear that pupils take the new technology for granted and that many of them not only have more sophisticated equipment at home, but that they spend hours using it, mostly for pleasure.

To that extent, the impact of new technology on schools is inevitable, but schools are also in a difficult position. There is a pressure of expectation on them, not just to respond to change but to lead it. Any reluctance to embrace change is quickly blamed and teachers come in for much criticism. This is not simply as a result of being slower to buy their own personal computers or showing less enthusiasm in pursuing the latest piece of equipment than the minority of converts. It has to do with the assumption from policy makers that they are not simply part of society but are there to shape it.

The difficulty for schools is that they face a number of contradictory demands: to teach skills that will be useful in employment; to inculcate social adaptability; to encourage personal learning beyond school; and to demonstrate what might be done with computers. In the end the central dilemma for schools in their response to these external pressures, comes down to a central question about the curriculum.

- Are schools essentially in the business of teaching pupils how to use computers?
- Or are schools mainly concerned with using ICT to deliver the curriculum?

Of course there is overlap between the two, but there are also many implications. Either of these propositions conjures up different schools than the traditional ones we are accustomed to and which are still promoted by the government through its rigid National Curriculum and plethora of tests and targets. If the school were to devote all its attention to teaching pupils about ICT, that would put the emphasis on pupils subsequently gaining access to information by themselves. If the school were to present the curriculum to a greater degree through the new technologies, that would also place teachers and students in a new position. Some would argue that the availability of information online, rather than through the teacher, already fundamentally changes the teacher–student relationship.

In the list of demands about the different uses to be made of ICT, It is clear that the policy is for schools to do both things at the same time: to teach computing, and to use computer programs in as wide an array of subjects as possible. This is difficult, not just because of the lack of resources, whether of computers or space, but because of the conflicting motivations beneath each endeavour. In all the cajoling of policy announcements, there has been little sign of understanding of the actual complexities for schools.

Even at the most basic levels there have been different approaches to ICT in education. One is the academic intention of learning about computers. Another is the cross-curricular desire to learn from computers. Yet another is the vocational aspect of learning with computers (Al-Haile 1994). Those who argue that the reason for the importance of computers lies in the government targets for vocational skills in the workplace would suggest that ICT might first be seen as an isolated subject but that this would soon be taken over by an integrated project approach and then be an integral part of the normal curriculum (Cole 1990).

As with other new technologies, the same people and organizations can at once take computers for granted and be made aware of them positively or negatively. Reactions to change are always a mixture of suspicion and reaction as well as unselfconscious use of new technologies. There is no new invention, for example the railways, that was not quickly made use of as well as deplored, sometimes by the same people.

In the complex reactions of schools to new technology there could be deemed to be three distinct roles: that of embracing education in technology as an intangible asset; that of using educational technology as a tool to create knowledge; and that of seeing it as a lever for other investment (Karen et al. 1998).

Educational technology is an asset that can be used in teaching, in the development of new resource bases and as a different means of enabling pupil– teacher interactions. As a tool, it can create new databases and new educational approaches, as well as new means of communication. As a lever for other investment, it can create connections with other institutions and market itself. We can see some of the results of this process in the way that schools are learning to present themselves. The growing tendency for schools to market themselves and to create mission statements is both a result of the government's implied policy of privatization, individualization and competition, and the result of the means that ICT makes available.

Underlying all these approaches is the norm of greater efficiency. This might not result in greater savings, but the advent of new technology does cause expectations that the school's system of communication and record-keeping, let alone the way it presents itself, should be slicker and more streamlined. Market forces are closely allied to new technology. This suggests that the same competitive edge that is brought to the private sector should be applied to schools.

> To achieve the full benefits inherent in this concept, instructional materials and practices must be designed with careful attention to the attainment of explicitly stated, behaviourally defined educational goals. Programmed learning sequences must be developed through procedures that include systematic tryout and progressive revisions based on the analysis of student behaviour. (Glaser et al. 1996, p. 3)

This is a clear statement of a new kind of expectation of schools, that they should be constantly testing themselves, trying things out. The new technology is envisaged as exerting the same creative pressure for experimentation and adaptation as in any private enterprise.

This sounds good, but does not comply with that other great imperative for schools, to conform to the National Curriculum and the many statutory orders. Marketing depends on the product and the product is tested in terms of SAT results and examination grades, inspection and league tables. The pressure to present the core curriculum of English and Maths (and Science) militates against creative uses of new technology. If there is great stress on covering a curriculum, there will always be less time for anything that gets in the way of this core business, like alternative approaches or additional resources.

Schools are expected to use computers in a variety of ways, some of them, given the resources, contradictory. While they are not (at least yet) explicitly judged on their use of ICT, but rather on traditional results, they are expected to be not only up to date, but also carrying the new technology forward with conviction. They are expected to make full use of what is available within their teaching and management practices, but they are also supposed to draw attention to the technology itself, to make their pupils and staff computer literate.

Since 1989, the government, through its main educational department (it is hard to keep astride of all the changes to nomenclature and acronyms) has stated various aims for ICT in schools. One is to enrich learning throughout the curriculum, to see it embedded in all subjects, to allow more collaborative and independent study (as long as the pupils pass the tests). Another is to give pupils confidence and pleasure in using ICT, so that they can master the techniques (although this is not tested). The third is to encourage flexibility and openness of mind, with an awareness of the needs of society (even if this is centred on the quickening pace of technological change). The fourth is to harness ICT to help pupils with special educational needs, and the fifth is to help pupils themselves design systems for solving problems.

Such aims draw attention to the fact that ICT is both a subject in its own right and the means to an end. It is something to be studied but also used. The question is whether it is a body of knowledge or a skill, a question that penetrates all parts of the curriculum. However, ICT is different in that it makes an impact on all parts of the formal curriculum is well as having subtle effects on the hidden curriculum.

In attempting to unravel the complexities many writers make a distinction between:

- learning about computers;
- learning from computers; and
- learning with computers.

During the 1970s and 1980s computer studies was one of the fastest-growing subjects in the country. There was a fascination with what the computer could do, and a sense of mastering something mysterious, powerful and resisted by others. Computer atudies had its particular adherents and became a popular alternative choice of pupils. It also became an examination subject. The Alvey report of 1982 urged a supply of highly trained graduates to teach computer studies in school. It had become a subject in its own right, taught by specialists, although their numbers remained low.

The teaching of computer studies created demand for up-to-date equipment and specialist resources, including a dedicated space. It was the ultimate vision of an educational technology resource, something seen as central and serving all aspects of the institution, but also something important in its own right. Instead of becoming a means of enhancing all aspects of the curriculum, ICT tended to be seen as another specialism, as another subject.

In computer studies there was always a tension between those who saw it as servicing the needs of all pupils, as giving them an awareness of what the equipment is capable of, and those who became intrigued with its potential and wanted it to be studied at the highest level. There were those who felt that computers gave access to higher mathematical skills, that programming was a reason for study. Others felt that all students should be given at least an awareness of what ICT could do, its impact on society and on their own lives.

The Department of Education and Science (1989) promoted computing as a specialist study by asserting that it would help pupils understand the capabilities and limitations of a broad range of applications, and that it would teach its users industrial and commercial management. It was also stressed, as it would be for other subjects or disciplines, that it would introduce pupils to problem solving and reasoning and would extend the mental capabilities of all. Thus it was envisaged as a mixture of academic challenge, social awareness and, as important, the development of a useful skill.

Computer studies has been used in a range of ways, from computer appreciation courses through computer literacy to the study of programming, problem solving and logical thinking. It draws attention to the question of whether it is a subject in its own right, or whether it is to be used in the service of other subjects (Loveless 2002). The underlying question, however, is whether it teaches those essential skills that are the basis of all subjects, logical thinking, the weighing of evidence and the application of ideas.

Before the development of the microchip there was a time when thinking about ICT centred not so much on its potential in everyday lives or access to the World Wide Web of information, but on the fact that programming demanded particular skills (Papert 1993). Since computer programs are sequences of separate instructions, the learning of a new kind of language was supposed to teach logic and problem solving. Programs such as LOGO were promoted as teaching the art of dividing large problems into smaller ones and providing an environment in which experimental solutions could be easily tested.

> There is an active group of educationalists who argue that learning to program is an ideal way of learning to think. (Underwood and Underwood 1990, p. 3)

Such a strong beliefs tended to fade away to be replaced by the use of word processing and spreadsheets. The databases that made the study fascinating lay not in the head of the programmer, but in the technology itself. The ubiquity of ICT makes it rather different from a specialist subject. Students who have difficulty with problem solving are not finding themselves particularly aided by computers (Freedman 1999).

Computer assisted learning (CAL) is a different approach from computer studies. When it was first introduced, it was considered a direct threat to teachers. With the rise of microcomputers such attitudes have changed since there is no longer that aspect of specialism and control. The belief in CAL is based on the idea that it augments, rather than supplants, traditional teaching methods, that it can efficiently provide remedial and individual instruction, that it presents enriched material in a cost-effective way and that it affords on-demand learning (Barker and Yeates 1985). This makes it sound like the ideal teacher, not a replacement, but a more than useful assistant.

In CAL the computer is a medium of instruction for a variety of subjects, rather than the subject of study in its own right. The question is what level of knowledge of computers do people need to have in order to make use of this rich resource? Any study of learning reminds us that it is not a simple process, but with many layers, from motor skills to verbal and visual imaging and cognition. Computer-assisted learning is depicted as having many applications. If computers are "teaching tools" then what they will deliver is not a theory of intelligence but different forms through which it can be manifested. Problem-solving is one clear example.

There are, however, some traditional aspects of teaching in which computers are seen to be helpful. The irony is that some of these are the most traditional of skills like "drill and practice" (Heinich et al. 1989). Rather than attempting to discover more creative endeavours, and before all possibilities of the Internet could have been accessed by schools, the use of computers was considered as a subject that consisted of "teaching tools" (Chuah 1987). Computers were considered to be an additional support, like a teaching assistant, to reinforce traditional aspects of formal learning. In the 1980s, and it is an attitude that still lingers, drill in practice programs were considered to be the easiest way of developing basic concepts and skills. Heinich et al. (1989) specifically targeted such practices as useful in mathematics, but also in modern languages, with vocabulary exercises and translation practices.

Even with the established subject boundaries, the computer was initially associated with the use of rote learning, with being able to make up in mechanical exercises that the teacher would otherwise have to undertake. Such an assumption overlapped with the concept of computer skills, the manipulation of keyboards and the fact that there is a least one aspect of ICT that is still closely linked to mechanical skills, namely the ability to type. There were pressing demands on more than knowing how to format and create spreadsheets.

The easiest form of computer-assisted instruction lies in the form of drills. As Chandler said,

> It is easier to produce software which reduces "learning" to a mechanical activity than it is to produce a tool which meets genuine needs. (Chandler 1984, p. 43)

The earliest and longest established uses of computer skills lay, therefore, in the use of reinforcement in exercises, in practice. In programs for spelling mistakes, punctuation and grammar, the computer was at once seen as useful as if it were a more practical and efficient type of learning machine. The computer was understood as a behaviourist tool.

To some extent, therefore, the pupils tended to associate computers with routine exercises rather than exploratory means of learning. While at home they might enter the fantasy worlds of games, making guesses and decisions, with quick psychomotor responses and fast judgments, but in school the uses of computers suggested something quite different.

In the earlier days of ICT, there were many commentators, as we have seen, who expressed great expectations in the potential of computers. This belief was in direct contradiction to the actual practices at the time, to the way that computers were actually being introduced. Those who were fascinated by programming were so deeply caught up in the exploration of computer logic that they were unable to convey their convictions to those to whom they demonstrated. The potential was there but seemed a far cry from the realities of the classroom.

The reason for the enthusiasm of the computer specialists was that the time when the computer was first seen as a tool of great potential was also one in which there was much emphasis on more creative ways of learning. The technology or resource centre was not enough in itself. The real change would be the way in which pupils made use of it. There were voices expounding the importance of inquiry or setting the pupil interesting tasks and encouraging them to find answers for themselves. The new technology that gave them the means to do this seemed like a godsend.

One of the developments of new methods of inquiry was the use of simulations. Again, this was an area in which the computer was assumed to be paramount. All these hopes in new modes of learning preceded the National Curriculum, with its monumental array of precise facts to be learned at particular key stages. There was always going to be a clash between the ideals of exploratory work, and the implacable demands of a formal curriculum.

Those who wanted to stress students' commitment to the excitement of learning saw simulations as a way of combining pleasure and understanding. Here the computer would be important.

> Within CAL, computer simulation is one of the most important modes of use and simulation means working with the models of a specific system. (Joachim and Wedekind 1982, p. 145)

The computer could supply mathematical models and generate interactivity. In contrast with the drills of practising, CAL, as opposed to learning about computers, was to provide simulation, the mastery of concepts and discovery learning. The belief was that simulations through the virtual world of the computer could provide the means to study the behaviour of systems in a way that would be impossible in the classroom. The potential lay in the exploration of the unknown, not in the mastery of a given curriculum.

The best example of simulations is games, a contrasting world of hyperactivity and different sorts of challenge. There are many who believe that this almost alternative world of learning provides more than empty-minded pleasure. The simulations that computer experts had in mind were earnest endeavours in problem solving, but we now see almost all that expertise devoted to games. Whilst there is the possibility that the interest of pupils can be fostered by the use of games, they themselves believe that they learn skills about the real world likes driving skills or controlling aircraft (Downes 1999). Alongside these mechanical abilities is the potential to solve problems and to develop perseverance, memory and imagination (Monteith 2000).

However the computer is used, for simulations or practice, it depends on a single, interactive process with an individual. While we more often see people sharing the same workstation, the culture of the computer remains that of the individual tutor rather than the collective teacher. Each student's progress can be checked and recorded. The computer in this mode is seen like a patient mentor to teach skills consistent with the rate of the student's capacity. It is supposed to provide systematic structure, implying behaviourist models of accumulated skills. Most programs keep a record of the student's progress; some can respond to individual needs, as well as the rate of learning. There has long been a belief that the tutorial program represents technology's way of providing each pupil with individual support that is patient and responsive to needs.

It is much easier to provide programs that rehearse well-known concepts or repeat established skills. It is far more difficult to create the kind of program that can by itself replicate the role of a teacher. Computer-based instruction was supposed to teach concepts and introduce new material and procedures in a must-provide practice (Criswell 1989). Such sophistication suggested that the programs provided could be like a substitute for teachers but this could only be so if the learning was passive (Willis et al. 1983). One of the consistent difficulties that has been encountered is that there are few examples of programmed learning that can manage without the intervention of a teacher. Like following a manual in setting up new systems, the mysteries of instruction can remain impossible unless there is extra advice and encouragement. The result is that many tutorial programs were and remain little more than programmed instruction books presented electronically, rather than in printed form.

Learning *about* computers was considered the first essential. Learning *from* computers has been seen as something to be striven for, making use of all the potential in giving instructions, testing skills and rehearsing what is known. Learning *with* computers is another dimension. Learning *with* computers is envisaged as teaching pupils programming, such as LOGO, using problem-solving, modelling and handling given information. This, again, is the goal of individualized tuition, but one in which the pupil has more of a command over the material he or she is dealing with.

For most people, and in most schools, computers are simply tools. They efficiently carry out tasks such as calculating and printing. Without the Internet and access to large resources, the computer can only remain a tool, however fast and efficient. Word processing, spreadsheets, databases, graphics and desk-top publishing might vary in sophistication but they are all tools, not cultural ones but practical. The pressure to revert to the most obvious applications of technology are great, and are not just a reflection of the nature of computers or of the habits of the classroom but of the functions of schooling and what they are supposed to achieve. This is a matter of tests scores, particularly in core subjects. It is therefore no surprise the ICT is seen as the least "well taught" of National Curriculum subjects. Inspectors report substantial underachievement. From 1998, ICT was an additional subject in the National Curriculum, not a skill, not an extra, but a *subject* to be inspected.

From the student's point of view, however, there are still possibilities in ICT that the usual practices do not take up. The potential of the computer, as they are aware, is not only that it can instruct and reveal, but that it can conjecture and emancipate. It can be seen as a machine narrowly focused on mechanical skills and drills. It can also be experienced as an entry into different worlds, not just the enclosed fantasy ones of games, but also the larger connections with the outside world. Whilst students are aware of blogging and chat rooms, they also have to recognize the potential of access to a great deal of information, even if some of it is forbidden.

The question is the extent to which all the excitement of computers and new communications systems, together with access to games and sources of information, from Google, Ask Jeeves and Wikipedia, translates into the systems of schooling. From those wedded to the potential of ICT, there is no sharp contrast between the excitement of discovery on the one hand and the mechanics of learning on the other. The way in which computers are presented, even if only in terms of potential, is that of exciting interactivity. LOGO can provide the user with immediate feedback on individual instructions, the "opportunity for the investigative approach to solving problems and development in the complexity of giving and modifying instructions. It also offers the chance of children to engage in a process, which they can relate to the real world" (Monteith 2000, p. 135).

The "opportunity" is both to connect to the ways they would use the computer at home and to see the same kind of interest taking place in the school setting. In school, however, it can be difficult to let students do what they want with their search engines. What is learnt has to be in the service of the academic curriculum. Computers, then, need to function in ways that will clearly demonstrate formal learning. Modelling is presented as something which "encourages the children to create instructions, to control events and see the consequences of their actions in real or imaginary situations" (Loveless 1995, p. 16). The National Curriculum makes the evaluation of real or imagined situations one of the attainment targets. As Papert (1980), points out, LOGO is the most famous example of modelling, but the idea of it as a way of learning across the curriculum is not widely supported (Somekh and Niki 1997).

If modelling is a particularly potent part of ICT, the most ubiquitous form lies in communication. In this way, computers replace other forms of writing, for example by letter; e-mail and access to chat rooms are a parallel to text messaging, a new form of communication, but with the implications of starting a new kind of language. Word processing can create all kinds of interesting documents and is a most practical means of communication. It can also be a chore. The crucial point, from students' points of view, is to have a purpose. There is no point in a skill without an outcome. The problem for many educational commentators on computing is that they point to the potential of ICT in such a way as to suggest private uses and individual interests.

> We enter an information age in which it is said that [technological] technology will penetrate every aspect of our lives from love letters to education, business transactions to personal communications, and there is a growing interest in how, and if children are learning to use these new technologies. (Science Direct 2001, p. 2)

The question should not be "if" children are using these new technologies, but where and how. The "penetration" into every aspect of people's lives lists education as just one of the many fields. Is this, indeed, how it should be perceived, as simply one amongst many examples of where new communication systems can be enjoyed?

The problem is that there has been for some time a strong urge to make schools take on the technologies not as something natural but as something forced upon them. Without any commensurate idea of changing the nature of schooling, ICT has been to many schools an additional burden, another aspect of the overcrowded curriculum, rather than an excitement. It might be a challenge, but is not one that has been chosen or sought out.

It is because of its ubiquity, as well as its potential, that so much emotional and intellectual investment has been made in ICT in schools. There is a contradiction at the heart of this. New communication systems are essential to the world of commerce. At the same time much of such commerce is to do with entertainment, with new systems for downloading games and playing music. The students at school take the whole of this environment for granted. It is a natural part of life, not something that they have to be cajoled into using. And then, at school, the whole matter becomes serious. They have to look at computers in a new kind of way.

The great potential of computing in education has been promulgated for years, but the significant developments in the technology have been commercial ones, for entertainment rather than for the sake of learning. When the power of computing has been put to academic use, as in the Genome projects, it has been as a tool in the service of thinking, not as an educational device. Yet schools are, as in the National Grid for Learning, expected not only to make the use of the potential of communication, but also to apply all kinds of new types of programmed learning, not in place of, but in addition to, the rest of the curriculum.

The government always stresses the importance of a skilled workforce. This includes the skills that make students computer literate and adaptable to the demands of the workplace either in the direct application to manufacturing as in robotics, or in the new offices that support commercial activities. If schools were seen simply as places where employment skills were fostered, the way in which computing needed to be taught would be clear. There is still a strong sense that computing could change education itself.

There are many examples of small-scale endeavours to use software in an interesting way, where the learner's enjoyment, motivation and commitment to learn is enhanced (Phillips and Pearson 1997). ICT can in itself be used to encourage pupils to create their own learning and work in groups on tasks that combine different elements as in a jigsaw (Perkins 2001). The potential is undoubtedly there, but such techniques are peripheral to the main developments in the commercial sphere, and not in the mainstream of the National Curriculum. That pupils can be given independence and encouraged to think for themselves is clear, but these examples are small in scale. There are few indications, even in technological academies, that there is a fundamental shift in approaches to learning.

Schools are in a difficult position. ICT skills are associated with entertainment rather than work – until it comes to employment. The National Curriculum, and the machinery of testing, puts computers at the service of the academic enterprise, not at the forefront – until it comes to prizes for good teaching in which ICT is the *sine qua non*. There are many contradictory pressures. The most important one is, however, that central conundrum of whether there is a need to study computers as a skill or whether the whole point of ICT is the use of computers in the service of academic subjects. Are computers an academic study or a tool to be used?

Conclusions

It is often remarked that the young handle information technology in a way that is easy and familiar, and more sophisticated than that of their elders. They make use of the technology in an everyday way, on the mobile phone, listening to music, sending text messages and accessing blogging sites. They carry this familiarity into school, but school makes quite different demands.

Schools face many dilemmas in their approaches to ICT. Apart from a lack of resources, they are not clear about what is expected of them. There are contradictory demands. Should computers be used for simulations, games and modelling? Should the emphasis be on rote learning and repeated exercises?

The main tension for schools is the question of whether they are there to teach computing or to use computer programs to teach other subjects. Is the computer a tool to be mastered, as something that will one day be used at work, or is it at the service of "delivering" the National Curriculum? It is hard for schools to recognize the creative potential of computers when there is such an insistence on testing and on outcomes that are measured by constant testing.

Chapter 3
Research on Information Technology

When a new technology is introduced all the attention is placed naturally on its operation, on how it can be most efficiently used. The aspirations for making the best of the opportunity are many, even if they are contradictory. When there are diversions from the welcoming of the new technology, they come in the form of either outright opposition or mute resistance.

Most of the research explores the potential of the technology by testing and experimenting with new programs. In the flurry of excitement and the desire to demonstrate what can be done, the reactions of all the users are rarely taken into account. There are few examples of the consideration of the effects of computers in actual institutions and very rarely is there an attempt to gather empirical evidence, even of the "before" and "after" kind. This lack of data partly comes about because the assumption is that the technology cannot be questioned and any doubts about is efficacy are a sign of a kind of Ludditism.

There are many examples of the impact of new technology described after the event and there are several interesting theories about the effects of new media, notably that by McLuhan, who made fashionable the notion that the medium was not just a conduit of an idea but becomes the "message" itself. Anything that is being communicated is not pure in itself but is contaminated and affected by the technological means through which it is transmitted. He argued the point that print technology, with its repetition of the same action, not only gave rise to the idea of factory output, where the production line as an exactly replicated system became the norm, but also affected fundamentally the way people think. Just as the warm collective embrace of the oral tradition was replaced by mechanical print, so were we about to see a kind of reversal to a different mode of thinking through the introduction of the new technologies. Mass communication was seen not just as a means of conveying information, in which the information itself made an impact, but also as a new style of thinking and feeling.

If print technology gave rise to the idea of a book as a repeatable object rather than each illuminated manuscript being as individual as a work of art, the development of steam and its application to steam presses led to many changes to styles of living. Railways transformed business and leisure in ways that were quickly understood and made use of at the time, even by those whose personal aspirations, like Pugin, might seem to run counter to such "modern" notions. Whilst some might feel threatened, from landowners to canal boat operators, the potential was clear to see.

The effects were another matter. We have already pointed out the complexity of results in the distribution of cheap printed material with both a rise in the number of people who seized on the educational possibilities and the more significant creation of a new public thirst for mass entertainment.

This division of effects is important. A new technology will be embraced with passion by some and taken for granted for others; it will offer opportunities both for greater learning and understanding, and for the appeal to lower common denominators. New technology is democratic. Its spread and ubiquity mean it can be used in a variety of ways. One can compare the past to the present but at the time people rarely think about the consequences for the future.

The future is another country. When television was first introduced, the immediate thoughts were on its educative potential, the transfer of images to a mass audience, but many of the possible effects were only considered when they had already had a huge impact. Both in the United States and in the United Kingdom there were early attempts to gauge the effects of the introduction of television (Schramm et al. 1961, Himmelweit et al. 1958). These surveys covered the extent of its use, the kinds of programs people watched, the amount they watched and when. It was only later that greater consideration was given to audience reactions, to the ways in which people used, as well as learned from, television (Cullingford, 1984). The problem was that many people wanted to exaggerate either the terrible effects of television or its entirely beneficial ones. They were motivated to prove a point that they already believed. They were not interested in empirical research that would involve individuals and their responses.

Television is now so taken for granted there is little of the same excitement or apprehension about it. While use is still made of its distance learning potential and many educative programs, the audience figures demonstrate its most popular appeal. Its uses are many. It conveys news and can reveal information in an effective way. The overlap between entertainment and instruction is always apparent, as in programs for the very young. It can be looked at closely, or as a kind of childminder to keep people quiet. Above all, it justifies itself and is used because it is entertaining.

As with the introduction of other technologies, the development of computing did not happen suddenly at one time. Indeed, the development from the mainframe to the microchip, and from that to laptops, has shown such an increase in power that in just a few years the advances have been as extensive as the far longer and slower development of the railways or print technology. Even more significant is the effect that computing has had on other technologies, including the operation of railways and the production of books.

The advent of information technology has evoked a sense of wonder but it has also embedded itself so deeply in people's lives and habits that it is difficult to grasp its significance. This has meant that, while there has been a great deal of attention given by academics to the subject, much of this has been given to the programs, the positive uses of technology, rather than the empirical evidence. The texts that comment on the use of ICT acknowledge the paucity of empirical research. This is understandable. It is very difficult to narrow down the subject, for example, the uses of the World Wide Web, or blogging or games machines. How can one measure the effects of using mobile phones on the way people communicate, or their habits and their conduct? Finding out what psychological differences such devices make is complex. Those who have had research grants, and there are many of these to do with computers, have to some extent looked at cultural indicators or the use of concept mapping – any endeavour which the computer enables – but empirical studies of the uses of computers, rather than the success of different programs, are few and far between.

The research that has taken place is largely about the programs themselves, how they are designed and what they look like. They vary greatly. The main research energy has been placed on how to develop good programs and how to test them. The testing that has taken place, often in higher education, has tended to be on the uses made of blackboard and other technologies that are available for individual and distance learning.

The belief in the potential of ICT has continued but has been joined by practical demonstrations of its uses. The creative employment of programs in the ways in which students can communicate with each other and with the tutors has made a real difference to the experience of learning (Thelwell 2008). There is also a continuing belief in the power of the individual to access learning and to work more independently. At the same time, one of the inescapable conclusions of the research that has taken place is that ICT enables but does not replace the teacher.

This means that the same organizations for education, schools, colleges and universities survive. They might be subtly different, and they certainly manifest the use of computers in all kinds of ways from cataloguing and assessment to marketing, but they are still places where people gather, where learning is centred, where teaching is organized. Indeed, one could argue that schools are more significant than ever. There might be different types and the whole hierarchy of successes and failures, but the National Curriculum and a regime of inspections as well as government controls underline the importance given to institutions as accountable, complete and hermeneutic.

Despite examples of distance learning, like the Open University, the programs and methods that have been developed by individual teachers are still based on the same institutions. One of the great dilemmas for schools is the abiding belief in their hegenomy as well as their accountability and the constant reminder that ICT gives a potential for completely different relationships between teachers and learners and for far greater communication between institutions. Looking at the research on programming, and on e-mail within educational establishments, we are reminded that attention is always on the exploitation of ICT and the uses of it made by students rather than the effects.

The question that is rarely addressed concerns the more profound, long-term differences made by the technology. Part of this question is whether ICT has made a difference to the experience of schooling. The theoretical debates about the different purposes and uses of the technology remain, but what do these mean in the lives of the pupils? Their awareness of ICT is clear, but does the excitement about its potential for learning make a difference to them?

The research reported here is unusual, if not unique. It explores the uses of the ICT from the point of view of secondary school pupils. It explores the way computers are used in school, and what the pupils think of their experience. It does not set out to preach the virtues and potential of ICT. It does not start with the hypothesis that the new technology is the best thing to happen for years. Nor does it seek to undermine what so many people take for granted. It simply asks about the evidence. After all the hype, what is actually happening in schools? Has ICT made a major impact?

To explore such questions means going into some depth. The questionnaire survey, however useful, could never in itself find out exactly what is going on from day to day, especially in the reactions and ideas of students. Whatever and however many hypothetical questions were formulated, they could never unpick the complexity, or the disparity, or the uniformity of students' experiences. The research is about ICT and is also about its context. It allows the students' individual experience at home as well as school and does not make judgments about individual teachers or programs.

For the results to have implications for all schools, a representative sample of secondary schools was chosen to allow for differences in socio-economic intake, amount of resources and other variables that make schools different.

The first school (A) was a mixed secondary of 1260 pupils with a sixth form, although some of the more able pupils in the area were able to go to one of three local selective grammar schools. While the overall attainment at entry was below average, the school was improving its reputation, and on the OFSTED score, "improving". The sixth form retained half the students and 10% came from other schools. The school had more pupils with special educational needs than usual. It had won several awards.

School B was much smaller, with 490 students. Some 35% of the pupils were identified as having special educational needs, well above the national average. The proportion of pupils speaking English as a second language was also high. A total of 50% of the pupils were entitled to free school meals. The school had difficulties in recruiting staff.

School C was also an 11–16 school, of 860 pupils. It had a good reputation for dealing with pupils with special educational needs. One-third of the pupils were from a minority ethnic background, mainly Pakistani or Caribbean. Students' attainment at entry was below average; the turnover was high. It was a specialist Sports College of long standing and much used by the community. It had also won several awards.

School D was a secondary school for 11- to 16-year-old pupils, with 760 students. Its proportion of special educational needs children was high and it had lower than average standards than the national norm, but was improving. Its intake included about one-third from minority ethnic groups.

School E had 1437 students with 205 pupils in the sixth form, which was expanding. Its intake came from a mixture of private and local authority housing and had about 10% of pupils for whom English was not their first language.

School F was a secondary school of about 1300 pupils. While the school catered for the full attainment range, most pupils went on for further study. It was a specialist Technology College and had gained a number of achievement awards, including becoming a Beacon school. It was involved in many extracurricular activities, including the Duke of Edinburgh's award scheme.

Each school was different in intake, ethos, culture and attainment. Each school had a different challenge, including the differences in socio-economic status, special educational needs and the challenge of language and home background. Even the briefest of such outlines is a reminder of the diversity of challenges and gives one pause about the notion of league tables, attainment targets and their inspectorial imperatives. Even the most obvious parameters of differences suggest the crucial contrasts, the absence or presence of a sixth form, the involvement of and reputation with the local community and the degree to which they are deemed to be successful. A significant number had won prizes in terms of awards. They were recognized to be doing exceptionally well, but the challenges they faced are clear.

These schools were therefore clearly different, each one with its own internal organization and unique external challenges. As such, they are also typical. While we cannot subsume all schools into the same criteria, it is clear that these collectively represent a typical selection of schools. They were state schools, but some of them thought of themselves (like academies) as superior to the rest. Rather than a homogenous system, we are confronted with a contradiction, an implacably similar set of instructions, targets, tests and inspections and an indefatigable array of differences within the schools and their surroundings.

These six schools, then, can be deemed to be typical of the country as a whole. They are reflections both of their local communities and of the national policy that at the same time encourages diversity and specialism and enforces uniformity of targets and outcomes and of the curriculum through the inspection regime. What is most important, however, and rarely pursued in the educational provision, is the community that surrounds the school. We see in these representative schools a wide variety of social–economic circumstances. There were many pupils with special educational needs. There were a significant number of pupils from minority ethnic backgrounds.

None of these schools was especially privileged, although they differed greatly from each other. They were not chosen as being the schools most committed to ICT, although one was a specialist Technology College. The issues that they faced are the same as those other secondary schools face in terms of decisions about the delivery of the curriculum, pressure on the core curriculum and the needs of other initiatives that keep being thrust upon them.

In terms of ICT the dilemma is also the same. To what extent were the resources adequate for the expectations made of them? Were the computers centred on a specially resourced unit or were they scattered around the school? Was computing a generic subject, taught as such, or was it at the same time, or alternatively, spread between the various subjects? What was the school's philosophy about the use of computing; which of the many competing claims seemed to dominate? Were the schools devoted to academic or vocational outcomes?

The most significant differences lay, however, in the neighbourhoods and what they represented in terms of parental support and previous educational achievement. This is a most important and often underrated issue, and affects schools profoundly. It is also the case with ICT. Many pupils will have better computers at home and at school (Cuthell 1999). Others will only experience the technology through devices such as games and telephones. The contrast between those technically tuned in and making use of all that technology offers and those who have to rely entirely on what they can derive from school is clear. The whole style of thinking and motivation will suggest significant differences.

The attitudes of the students which are reported here are therefore representative of a wide variety of backgrounds and circumstances. They are not representative of the selected elite, excited by and dedicated to the latest technologies, nor are they typical simply of the deprived, who have had little access to computing. The number of these is inevitably diminishing.

It is the students rather than the schools who are the centre of attention. It is what they say about their experience that matters. While the schools were observed, they were not being inspected. The judgments that pupils make might be about their particular school, but it is both the range of experiences and the uniformity of judgments, whatever their circumstances, that matter.

The six schools chosen as representing the broad band provision in terms of size, intake, outcomes, location and resources were all observed to see how they managed the delivery of ICT. The observations give a constant background to the more detailed reports of the students so that some correlations can be made between the types of experience they had and their personal views. The information gathered was about the way ICT was taught, in what circumstances and where. It was the students' behaviour that was observed rather than the prowess of the teachers. No judgment was made of the school and this is reiterated because in all literature that surrounds the introduction of ICT there is a constant emphasis on what *ought* to be and what schools *should* do. This work is about the reality, not the vision of what might be, and is therefore sympathetic to the dilemmas and choices teachers and schools make. It is only by understanding the reality of the circumstances that real changes can be made.

The centre of the exploration is in trying to understand the individual and shared experiences of the pupils. It is not is another manual on how to do things or arguments for particular resources and programs. There are studies about individual initiatives concerning approaches to distance learning, concerned with particular circumstances. The research is about the whole experience of school, in which ICT is embedded. In terms of ICT, the whole experience is far greater than the school itself. We are therefore dealing with the subject in terms of the lives of pupils; the attitudes formed and fostered by their overall experience. Given the ubiquitous nature of the new technology, it is impossible to treat it as an isolated school phenomenon. At the same time, the experience of ICT in school is dependent on the overall context of schooling.

The observations of the schools were combined with questionnaires and semi-structured interviews. The sample size depended on two factors, the first being to make sure that it was representative of the whole and the second that there was enough consistent evidence to demonstrate validity and reliability. In all, 310 pupils took part in the questionnaire surveys, and there were 29 semi-structured interviews. The pupils who took part were those who expressed some kind of interest in ICT as well as wanting to take part in the research and explain their opinions. There was such a large cohort to choose from that those who were most willing and interested still represented all the shades of background and all schools.

There are other places where research methods are fully documented (Haq 2006), but this survey reflects standard practice. Certain types of information lend themselves to be gathered in a quantitative way, such as different types of organization or teaching method. For details of attitudes, motivations and opinions, however, the only means of exploring the complexities in any depth is through ethnographic interview.

Both quantitative and quantitative techniques were not only piloted but arose directly from the observations. They were the means of going into greater depth about the different factors that seemed to affect the experience of ICT. The positive data was mostly confined to the uses of computers, and when and where lessons involving them took place. For the overall attitudes to the experience of school, semi-structured interviews were more appropriate.

The research question was a broad one (Sapsford and Jupp 1996), and did not rest on a narrow hypothesis. It emphasized that there was no desire to prove the efficacy or otherwise of distinct approaches to the delivery of ICT. The research question was open-minded, trying to find out without bias or prejudgment what the overall experience of ICT was for secondary school students, in particular in relationship to the rest of their experience.

The reason for this approach should be clear. Much of the research has been concerned with implicitly proving hypotheses, like exploring how computers can give access to more knowledge, analysing the benefits of distance learning or demonstrating how ICT leads to more individual learning. If there is any one large underlying hypothesis that is the starting point, it is one that has been reiterated over the years – the notion that ICT will inevitably change the nature of schooling, from the teaching of the curriculum to the organization of the classroom. This book explores whether, and how, schools have been affected by ICT and, more centrally, how and whether the students' lives have been changed by its introduction and use.

The context in which the pupils studied was important. The different schools varied in the amount of ICT resources but they did not vary greatly in terms of the approaches to teaching and learning. Two of the schools were very much better resourced than the others, an outcome to some extent of catchment area and school and district policy. Some of the schools tended to use the computer simply as a tool. While two of the schools were strongly resourced, two were clearly undersupplied and deficient in technology in comparison with the others.

The classes chosen for observation and the students used for the questionnaires and interviews represented the variety of schools and backgrounds, with a balance of gender. They were taken from year nine, and year ten. Any consistency in the findings is despite the variety of experiences and backgrounds of those taking part.

Conclusions

There is probably more funded research in education concerned with computers than any other kind. The choice of what is funded lies in the hands of government agencies and the control over what takes place is tight. The fact that ICT is of such interest might suggest that this is the direction in which policy makers are thinking.

This is only true up to a point. The research is targeted at the making of programs, at exploring new approaches to enhancing the experience of students; it engages interest because it attempts to be creative. What is does not do is to look more generally at the effects on computers on the people using them. The crucial subject that remains unexplored is the difference between the uses of computers, an essentially individual matter, and the organization of schools, as collective and social.

Government policy, enshrined in the National Curriculum, insists that all schools have the same curriculum, the same targets and the same tests. The schools that were included in this research demonstrated how different and varied they were, despite the statutory orders. They varied not just in the resources available to them, and their handling of them, but in their circumstances, their neighbourhoods and their intakes. They all faced similar pressures and were all doing their best to be positive about ICT, but were handling the pressures in different ways.

Chapter 4
Students' Attitudes to Computers: The Experience at Home

Students' attitudes to computers in school are affected by their experience at home. They depend partly on the contrasts in the types of equipment, partly on the uses to which the technology is put and partly on the conditions in which it is used. Computers are essential to everyday actions that people take for granted, like most commercial transactions. The credit card has replaced the money that Marshall McLuhan long ago called "the credit card of the poor". It does not need the deliberate use of eBay or money transfers for people to be aware of the centrality of the Internet. Computers are also associated with the many games that are not only available but popular. Those who keep reiterating the adage that only the young can master technology are drawing inadvertent attention to the fact that computers are a natural part of their lives.

The kind of familiarity that the pupils have with ICT is in direct contrast to the experience of school. Taking something from granted, using it or playing games with it is not the same as studying. At school, the very fact that computers are to be studied as well as used creates in itself a novelty. The question is what kind of novelty this might be. If the pupils have had a great deal of experience, and use ICT at home, then they should be curious about what might be made new for them in the more erudite world of school. They might be aware of the great potential for computers in the teaching of a range of subjects or have had experience, not only through the World Wide Web, but also through television, of the rich presentations of historical facts, scientific wonders and well-illustrated accounts of other subjects. If they are innocent of such technology at home they might arrive with either great hope or greater apprehension.

Whatever the students' experience, we should not underestimate their prior knowledge and awareness. Nor should we forget the significance of their overall attitudes to school. After several years of experience, the pupils will have formed certain expectations and assumptions about the school experience, both within and outside the classroom. If this is a stimulating and enjoyable experience, anything new or different will be met with approval and expectation. If the overall impression of school is of routine and boredom, it will be more difficult to stimulate their interest in anything.

It is this overall attitude to school, in which ICT is another subject, which is significant. All the messages about the way in which computers will transform learning depend on the assumption that schools will be radically different, they will be changed or that at least the working habits of pupils will be changed. The ways in which the new technology is used obviously depends on the context and the context must obviously be associated with the home, the personal workstation and personal pleasures and usefulness.

This is a study of ICT at school, and not about the ways in which programs are used at home for access to pleasure or knowledge. However, the wider context will always be significant. There is a marked connection between having computers at home and deriving pleasure from them. In the interface between home and school lie the "Out of School Clubs", where computers are associated overwhelmingly with fun and play. The pupils who attended such clubs were adamant that certain educational practices, particularly those to do with writing, should be avoided (Edward 2002). They were clear about the demarcation lines between home and school.

It is because of the psychological contrasts between home and school that the relationship between them is so important. While pupils associate home with freedom from constraints, with pleasure and relaxation, they are also aware that it is not quite so simple a contrast. They have homework to do, and many do all their real work at home, using school as a social centre where they hand in what they have done (Cuthell 1999). They also know that home is not either symbolically or actually a place where they are able to escape from all demands. They know that even there they are confronted with academic expectations (Cullingford 2007).

Nevertheless, the psychological conditions of home life are very different from the whole experience of school. One essential distinction is between the freedom of being an individual and the constraints of groups, which are a central part of school. Even when there is sibling rivalry, the relationships of the home are individual and iterative. The quality of the dialogue might vary significantly, but there is still that sense of individual conversation, encouraged rather than deplored (Heath 1983). In school, the demands of rules and organization create conditions of mass movements, of the control of groups. These can be for social and structural reasons, from classes to assemblies, or they can be for academic ones, the groups within classes for the sake of sharing resources, or for streaming in terms of ability. Whatever the reason, the experience of school is an experience of masses of people, in which the individual voice is subdued. This is true of the inner spaces between lessons and in the playground. Groups of whatever size matter when there are crowds of people. The whole social experience is different.

Computers, however, demand individual activity, and an iterative dialogue between the person and the machine. Whether it is a game to be played or a communication to be sought, and even if many others beyond the machine are involved, the essential connection is between the computer and the person. The individual always chooses when and at what pace to work. The individual is supposed to be in control. This can explain the very personal and embittered way in which frustrations are taken out on the screen.

The computer is part of the ethos of individuality that home provides. Even while there might be arguments about who is allowed to operate it at any one time, these arise because of the individuality of experience. No one is forced to use computers at home, and they enjoy it when they choose to do so.

There are fewer and fewer pupils who do not have a computer at home. Once it was a mark of the privileged to have access to ICT. Now it is a signal of deprivation not to possess a good computer, up-to-date and an essential part of the equipment of a home. Some 90% of the pupils made use of the computer at home, whether for games or for work. It is not just a matter of possession, but of utilizing the equipment. There could be students whose parents do not allow them access to a computer, but it is more likely that the 10% of pupils are those who do not have a computer at home. The computers in use were invariably PC Windows, with just three out of 276 using an Acorn or a Macintosh. In 90% of cases, the home computer was compatible with those used at school.

One problem for schools is that the computers they use are rarely, if ever, more up-to-date than those used at home. Indeed, there are times when the contrast is marked (Hollingworth and Eastman 1997). Schools do not have the resources to regularly update their equipment and so they cannot offer the pupils an obvious attraction. What the schools therefore depend on is demonstrating the different ways that ICT can be used beyond the mechanics of word-processing and the ephemera of games. Not only do pupils tend to have better equipment at home than in schools, but they also have better accessories such as graphics software, scanners and fax machines. They also usually own better equipment than their teachers do.

The availability of access to the computer is not the same as using it, but of the 90% of pupils who had a computer at home two-thirds said that they used it on a daily basis. The others used it less frequently, but only 5% used it as rarely as about once a month. When we learn how often pupils use a computer in school, this frequent use of it at home needs to be borne in mind.

Having access to the computer on a daily basis, however, is only the starting point for the different styles and amounts of computer usage. Of the pupils, 5% reported that they would spend up to one hour per day on the computerm and nearly 30% reported that they would spend, on average, between one and two hours per day. Another two-thirds noted that they would spend between two and three hours on the computer at home each day.

There were also those who spent larger amounts of time using the computer. Some 11% would engage with ICT for between three and four hours and 8% between five and six hours per day. This is a significant part of their lives, and shows not just the ubiquity but also the centrality of computers. Their uses are many since much of the entertainment lies in the technology, from games and music to videos and chat rooms. In the early days of television, researchers were astonished at the amount of time being spent watching it and they tended to conclude that active play was going to be replaced by passive entertainment, since there was so little time left in the day.

Computers offer so much more than television that it should be no surprise that people spend so much time with them. Not only do they have the demands from school to prepare their homework, but pupils also have the means to communicate, sometimes at great length, with their friends, and they also spend many hours in long and complex games. The use of computers is a central part of their lives and dominates the time they spend at home.

The amount of time that the pupils calculated they spent using computers at home was worked out on a daily basis, since this was easiest to calculate, and it made them realize how much they used computers. This contrasts with the amount of time spent on computers at school, which could only be calculated on a weekly basis. About 50% of the 310 pupils spent an hour per week on the computer. Another 31% spent two hours per week. The amount of contact with ICT in schools was drastically different. This also implies a different kind of usage. Perhaps the experience in school, if short, is more intense and more demanding. This is at least a possibility to be explored.

Computer use at home is not thought of in terms of the demands but of pleasure. There were many different uses of computers that the pupils commented on. The great majority used computers for playing games, for the Internet or e-mail. There were other uses as well, some to do with school work, like PowerPoint and spreadsheets. Some 40% reported "drawing pictures", but the main uses of computers were the obvious domestic ones of communication and pleasure.

The centrality of computers in pupils' lives lies partly in the time spent on games. There are educational games available as well as simulations, but even within school the games that the pupils like to play are strategy games, action games and sports-based games, and these are the kinds of activities, sometimes involving role-play, that they carry out at home. At home it is action games that are most popular, followed by strategy games. One might question how demanding some of these activities are, but they certainly are engaging and stimulating and some would argue that they teach distinct skills.

Whatever the level of skill involved, the games are very interesting. Only 1% of the pupils was not interested in playing computer games or found them boring, and a few more were not particularly engaged. There was a clear commitment and pleasure in playing games on the computer, a kind of activity and attitude that naturally contrasts with the experience of school. Computers at home were universally found "very interesting" or at least "interesting". At home, the computer is associated with pleasure and is a central activity in the daily lives of students .

One of the reasons for the pleasure derived from using a computer at home, given its availability, is its flexibility. The pupils all report that at home, even when they work, they work at their own pace. They are in control of what they wish to do. They decide when they want to work and when to play games. They can decide what to do and do not feel that there are time constraints. They also report that they have access to more interesting material. Both the conditions of use and the kinds of activities they do are preferable at home.

Home gives a sense of personal autonomy. They make their own decisions and feel they have their own space and time. Even when doing work, the home computer gives them the opportunity to present their work in a more sophisticated way, as well as giving them access to a wealth of material. Clearly, the computer is enjoyed at home, and is a source of real pleasure as well as an opportunity. The question remains what connection the home computer has to the learning demanded by school. That there are potential links is clear (Schall and Skeele 1995), but there is little research on the ways in which pupils' use of their own computers relates to that at school (*Educational Technology Review* 2002). There is evidence that pupils like to do the bulk of their work at home by themselves, but this is still work that is school-related. The relationship between games and schoolwork is another matter.

Pupils associate using the computer at home with pleasure. When they do so, they immediately contrast it with their attitudes to computers in school. Home provides freedom from constraint and escape from demands.

> At home, you are away from the stress of the teacher. (Boy, year nine)

Home is where there is less stress anyway, but it is also the place where there is freedom to work in an individual way, when work can be interspersed with entertainment, where one is allowed to walk away from the workplace or engage in conversation. Pupils can also work when they want to only at home.

> At school, they are a bit slow, but at home, you can go really on any website, if your mum is not in the room. At home you can play games. So I do like to use computers at home. (Boy, year nine)

Even if there are limitations to using a computer at home, these are not nearly as many as those of school, where the demands are so much greater. The variety of what is available at home is so much greater in a number of ways.

> At home, you can go on any website and in school they make you go on certain web sites, and if you are at home, you can go on like working web sites and then afterwards you can go on mini clips for games. You can get lots of different games and it's fun. (Boy, year nine)

The lack of constraints at home means in itself that computers will be found far more attractive. The fun lies not just in the games but in the ability to do whatever is wanted. There is a balance between work and play that is appealing. The pupils not only play games at home, but enjoy the fact that they can do so whenever they want to.

> In school, we just do work, typing things, but at home I play on computer games and talk to my friends on the Internet. (Boy, year nine)

It is the variety and choice that count. Apart from anything else there is both time available and the opportunity to talk to friends. While school is a social centre, and appreciated as a meeting place, it is at home that dialogue is allowed, even if it is through e-mail.

> You get more freedom at home. In school, you just have to do what you've been told to do. (Girl, year ten)

School gives the sense of external demands and control. Learning in such conditions is not something desired or sought after, but imposed.

> In school, you got to get some work done in about say 30 minutes. But at home you can do whatever you want to do. Like if you go on the Internet you can just keep on going through instead of going back to your work. You can keep on going, whatever you're doing. Teachers do not distract you. (Boy, year nine)

The demands of the National Curriculum result in a sense of a burden, the need to fulfil particular tasks. In these conditions, teachers can even be found a "distraction". The time that is available at home means that pupils can pursue a particular line of interest without interruption and can concentrate on the task in hand. It is not simply a matter of having the time to pursue other interests or to play games but of having time to do work properly.

The different conditions of using the computer at home mean that any activity is approached with more pleasurable anticipation. There is a sense of having time, of being able to add to a task the occasional distraction. Home, in fact, is the main place for computers.

> I use my computer at home, and most of the time I'm on the Internet. So I'm always talking to people on chat sites and stuff like that. The difference is, it's a different atmosphere, and you can relax at home. Sometimes you feel a bit tense in school. (Boy, year ten)

The computer at home is the source of relaxation and natural interest. The sense of privacy is itself important, for this is contrasted with a sense of surveillance with which all school is weighed down.

> Teachers are always watching you. You're supposed to be working all the time in lessons really. (Girl, year ten)

However interesting the material, the sense that there are targets and that they must be seen to be "on task" prevails.

> At home it easier because I got more time to use it. (Girl, year ten)

All the pupils who use computers at home talk about different kinds of freedom. This is a matter of having time, as well as being able to choose activities, and this explains how they can spend so long on the computer.

> There is a lot more freedom at home. You can do what you really want to do. And you can stay on the computers as long as you want to home. It is better at home. (Girl, year ten)

The home computer is not just a source of entertainment but a benchmark for what such technology can do. The work that is done at home can be fun. It is an individual activity, sought-after rather than forced. It is not just a matter of simple contrast between work and entertainment.

The home computer is often more sophisticated than those on offer in school.

> My computer at home is like better than the ones in school. Mine is new. (Girl, year nine)

More important is the association of computers with choice, with pursuing interests, with freedom from unwanted or unnecessary constraints.

> It's more private. You can write whatever you like. You haven't got teachers and people watching you all the time. (Girl, year nine)

The pupils associate computing with their own private experiences. They are making daily use of the technology as if he were the most natural thing to do.

The home computer is also associated in their minds with an alternative way of approaching work. Instead of set tasks and group activities, they find they have the freedom to explore what interests them. Indeed, this sense that the computer offers more in home conditions actually reflects on their schoolwork.

> At home, it is better because you can just learn more at home and at school, they don't teach you. (Boy, year nine)

The computer has become a symbol of what learning can be like and leads to greater reflection on the contrasting experience of school. In the light of these accumulated incidents, the tendency to reappraise what goes on in school is strong.

> Well at school, we just do work typing things but at home I play on computer games and talk my friends on the Internet. (Boy, year nine)

This might seem like self-indulgence, but it demonstrates to the pupils what computing offers. The exchange of information and day-to-day communication with their friends means that they know that ICT gives access to knowledge, and the possibilities of collaborative learning and mutual support. It also means that their curiosity can be placed in different directions.

It is the multiple uses of the computer that are appreciated. They are associated with flexibility and their accommodation to the desires of their users.

> If I am not doing my homework I like to go onto the Internet, looking at new music websites, and things like that, you know and finding out funny things. I can e-mail my friends. It's kind of faster really than writing a letter, because when you write a letter and sent it, it takes time. And if you're e-mailing your friends you can communicate better. (Girl, year ten)

The habit of "multi-tasking" is clearly associated with the Internet. It is possible to have several different things going on at once, juggling between a text message, seeing the news, hearing the latest songs and working on a task. The whole approach to the giving and receiving of information is different, where distraction distracts from distraction, where new forms of text message intersperse with more serious information, all at the same time. This speed of communication, and the fact that it can take place at any time, also makes this new world of communication and access to layers of different information full of potential change, in modes of thought as well as study.

Whether people actually "communicate better" remains a moot point, but they do so in different ways, probably shorter as well as faster, and probably with more people. The Internet provides hosts of acquaintances and details about people. It makes the world into a party full of chatter and, as in a party, one passes from one person to another. This can become so much a matter of course that it relates to more general attitudes to concentration than an intense dialogue. Such types of communication contrast with the *modus vivendi* of schools; while they can be taken into a school they are against the normal culture in which a school operates, with the concentration on one thing at a time surrounded by vast spaces of silence.

Pupils become accustomed to playing with sites, to exploring and changing from task to task. At home they can do this in an eclectic manner, at a variety of levels.

> Because if I was at home, I would like go onto the Internet and look at some sites, do what I wanna do. But in school, you are doing something totally different and sometimes I feel like that we do some stuff I couldn't understand why we're doing this. It's not even important. Most of the things we do in school is just boring, it's not interesting, it's not fun. That's what makes people not want to work in ITE. (Girl, year ten)

The opportunities to do what they want to do, when they feel like it, mean that their experience of home contrasts even more than ever with that of school. The constant and instant communication with friends is matched by immediate access to games and shows, to music and gossip. All types of information, presented in a similarly bright and breezy way, are available.

Against such a use of computers school would inevitably present a contrast.

> At home, you're free to do what you want. You're free to go on any like web
> pages. Like, you can play games and staff. At school we can't do that. I can use
> the Internet when I want to, and how I want to as well. (Girl, year ten)

It might not be a surprise that pupils are not allowed to use the equipment in school in the same way that they would at home. The equipment in school is in short supply so there can be no individual access. The students are struck by the fact that, although the computer remains the same kind of facility, one to which they are accustomed, and which they enjoy, it is used for a different purpose in a different way.

There are, then, a number of clear contrasts. At home the atmosphere is "relaxed", while at school there is a tendency to feel "tense". At home, there are multiple choices, not only between different activities, but between the amount of time to be spent on each. The time spent on computers at home is far longer and its significance greater.

> You get longer at home. You don't get into trouble for going on, something
> you're not supposed to. You can play games or listen to music, you can check
> your e-mails at home, which you don't do at school. (Girl, year ten)

While the computer is associated with pleasure, it is also used for work. This means that homework has a different feel, a task that can be done while being mitigated by other interests. The emphasis is then on the acquisition of information, and on its presentation.

The contrasts between the pleasures of computers and their more serious application can mean that each style of use is seen as different, even by parents.

> Well, I got a computer at home, but my mum and dad feel I should use computers
> in schools as best I can. They do let me use it at home if I've got to do my
> homework. (Girl, year ten)

This in itself suggests that the association made by computers in each place is different. The contrast is not just between hard or demanding work and the ease of entertainment but in the whole attitude shift both to learning and to general activity. The potential distinction between work and play is also exacerbated.

The prerequisite on schools to make use of ICT is against this background of an alternative world, often with better equipment, more facilities, more time, more flexibility and far more pleasure. What then do schools offer, and how do they present what they do?

Conclusions

Computers are a central part of the experience of home. Students come to school with a great deal of experience and clear attitudes. The computer is associated with pleasure, both private and shared. Students play games and choose music and various programs that they enjoy. They also are in touch with their friends through e-mail, and through access to websites.

The computer at home is there to respond to demands. It is an individual instrument, flexible and pleasurable. It offers choice and variety. It encourages an eclectic way of working and thinking. The computer is familiar and private, but it also offers access to the public realm.

Nothing could contrast with this more clearly than the experience of school. The school is marked out by the organization of groups. The emphasis is on the collective endeavour of classes. The freedom to seek out information is curtailed and the work is imposed on the students. The computer is no longer at the students' service but the other way round.

Chapter 5
Students' Attitudes to Computers and their Utility

The impressions of new technology and the attitudes that are formed towards them depend on the context in which they operate. There are contradictory opinions towards computers, welcoming the facilities and communication offered by ICT and deploring computers when they go wrong. People praise the ease with which transactions can be carried out and also worry about the amount of spam and the criminal activities that are generated with their private actions exposed and contaminated. Attitudes to computers vary with their use as well as expectations. On one level, the ubiquity of computing is taken for granted, and unconsidered. On another, they are seen as difficult to comprehend, a challenge. When pupils talk about computers at home they are seen as a pleasure, a support to learning perhaps, but more a source of entertainment. In this context, attitudes are generally positive.

Such an attitude contrasts with the use of computers in schools and the distinction is clearly made. The impression that computers give in the school context can be quite different, another challenge or even a threat. At school, the curriculum is to be taken seriously. It is a matter of knowing how to learn and retain facts, having memory tested and skills reiterated and repeatedly practised.

The investment of belief in computers that pervades policy, and which affects schools, is powerful. This does not mean that it is shared by the pupils. What they think about computers depends on their attitudes to their futures and to the curriculum. While ICT might be full of possibilities, and these are experienced at home, this does not mean that they are seen to apply to school. The question is, given the contrast with the uses of their time at home, whether the attitudes towards computing as a subject and as an experience are nevertheless positive. An experience can be useful without being necessarily pleasurable. It can be recognized as significant even while it is resented. What then are the attitudes to computers in that context?

The first important point to note is that there was no strong antipathy to computers. The very fact that they were taken for granted meant that the basic assumption about them was positive. Just 3% thought that computers were a "waste of time". There was a distinction made between the utility of computers in themselves and the uses to which they were put in school. Some 15% of the pupils felt neutral about computers, not thinking them the best use of time, perhaps, but at least not a waste of it. The majority were far more positive. They felt that using a computer was a significant and beneficial thing to do; however long they spent on it, it was a sensible and useful act. The variety of tasks that computers represented meant that it was difficult to be wholly negative about them. Eight boys felt disgruntled about computing, but this extreme was balanced by a large percentage of boys who were extremely enthusiastic about using a computer. While the girls were also positive, more boys than girls declared a passionate interest in the uses and activities of computers.

The reasons for being positive about computers varied from making their work look better to seeing the necessity of learning about them for their future employment. The very fact that computers are an essential tool for modern business, as well as a source of entertainment, creates a sense that there is a need to be positive overall. There are few businesses, if any, that are not dependent on computing, partly because it is such an important means of communicating and gaining access to information, and partly because they speed up so many tasks. All office work has been transformed by computers (Khalid 2000). All the long drawn-out tasks of creating data and accumulating information, like numbers and calculations, have been fundamentally changed.

The pupils were asked whether they thought that computers save time. In the context in which they were placed the pupils thought of themselves and the work they did, without explicit reference to application in the workplace, of which they had limited knowledge. If the time spent using computers was useful, did they have a sense that it was time "well" spent, efficiently? A very small minority, just over 5%, could not see savings of time or their tasks being significantly speeded up by using the computer. The rest were positive, with half of the boys asserting that the computer saved a great deal of time and a third of the girls agreeing with this. However, there were difficulties in making distinctions between saving a "lot" of time and a "great deal" of time, or even "some" time. What matters is their sense of the sheer efficiency of computers.

There are all kinds of ways in which the efficiency of computers can help: in storing information, calculating and correcting and presenting the results. As Cuthell (1999) points out, pupils realize how much neater they can make their assignments, knowing how influential the appearance of work that is presented for marking is. There is a kind of competition in terms of presentation in a world where neatness is so important. However, the fact that computers are so efficient does not necessarily mean that pupils look at them with increased excitement and with a surge of adrenalin. Efficiency can mean routine.

A question was asked about the extent to which computers were found to be definitely exciting. Once again, the results were very positive. While half of the girls tended to be fairly neutral about the computer, it was only a small minority of about 6% who did not feel themselves to be stimulated by using a computer. The boys were again more positive in their views on computers, with over a third being very excited by them. Whatever the variety of their experiences, there was a strong belief that computers in themselves enhanced experiences. They were not just efficient and useful and exciting to use. The students' mindset was firmly on the side of ICT.

Given the amount of time spent on computers, and as a result of these views, was there ever a sense that the experience of using computers could be tiring? Many of the tasks can be fairly standard routines, and a significant number of demands made on the students can only be answered through the labour of word processing, so it would not be surprising if pupils were wearied by using computers. Few students said that they found using a computer tiring. Of this minority, the reasons they gave were significant. They cited psychomotor difficulties, of posture or strain on the eyes, rather than anything intrinsic to the computer itself. Some identified problems to the wrists or hands, and could blame the design of the keyboard, mouse or the chair as they showed themselves aware of the potential for injury from repetitive tasks. This in itself could come about because so much time can slip past unnoticed when one is involved with a computer.

Apart from those who had noticed some of the physical results of spending so much time in one position, with the eyes closely engaged on the screen and with small movements of the wrists and fingers, the attitudes to computing remained positive. The students asserted that computers did not cause tiredness. Some 80% of the pupils did not associate ICT with being weary at all; they did not feel tired of the task itself. There are, of course, certain things that computers offer which would never be linked to any kind of strain, from music to play games.

It is becoming clear that students' attitudes to computers are essentially positive. Is this an inevitable result of their experience or a response to the many presentations they will have encountered in which the virtues of computers are talked about positively? To what extent do they see computers as important in themselves? That they help, that they are efficient, is clear, but the students were asked about the significance of computers in their lives and, by implication, in the development of society. Nearly 90% asserted that using computers is important. Whether they like the experience in itself or not, this is a fact that they accept.

Even those who do not have computers at home know about their importance. Such received wisdom is derived both from the experience of people playing games, seeing advertisements and going past shops full of equipment, and from the constant cajoling of policy makers. Such a mixture of opinion and experience has its effect, and even those who might have had poor experiences with computers recognize the facts.

This awareness of the importance of computing even within the context of school is very important. It suggests a familiarity with, and awareness of, the transactions of the world. It means that students are an audience who do not need much convincing, who are ready to accept the significance of the subject. In order to assess the depth of this commitment, the students were asked a succession of subtly different questions with words like "usefulness" and "worthwhile" added to the sense of importance. The aim was to try and make distinctions between the sense of utility, and the feeling of pleasure, between the assumption that computing is an inevitable part of the social and educational landscape and the feeling, still prevalent amongst commentators, of a sense of wonder.

"Worthwhile" can mean all kinds of things, but it does elicit the feeling of general benevolence. Something can be gained in using the computer. Only five students reported that they did not find using computers worthwhile. However seriously the computer is taken, or however dismissively it is used, students clearly appreciated its multifarious values.

The reasons for this positive response can be many, both as a result of public pressure and private satisfaction. The students were therefore asked about whether they viewed computing more as a means of entertainment or a significant factor in their future careers. The computer at school could, after all, be simply associated with what they ought to know. The home computer might be alternatively significant, simply because there is no pressure to take it too seriously.

The assumption by the government, in its sponsorship of ICT, is that a skilled workforce has to be aware of how to handle a computer; hence its place in the syllabus and the insistence that it should be learned for its own sake. One cannot argue against the importance of using computers, and this could be said to be done naturally and simply, without any sophistication attached to the making of new programs. Whether the students see the centrality of computers in their working lives is another matter.

The students were therefore asked to assess how helpful learning to use computers would be for their futures. They had no doubts that they felt it to be central. One girl and one boy thought it had no significance for their future careers. While one might assume that all are computer literate, the ways in which computers are used in the workplace can often mean more than simply carrying out standard tasks and functions. There are many manual jobs which do not demand the use of computers but all the students, whatever their background, saw the importance of using the computer in their future lives.

There is a range of possible attitudes to the centrality of computers, which are usually combined. They can be seen as a source of entertainment and a source of communication. This ability to exchange information and have access to it is central to people's private interests and essential to the workplace. While computers are the most important means of financial and stock control, not only in terms of storage but also in terms of databases and modelling, this does not mean that there is anything especially arcane in their usage. Many people are not aware of the peculiar significance of computing in their daily lives. It might be a wonder to the enthusiasts, but is taken for granted by ordinary users. To find the computer "useful" or "important" is not a simple matter of recognition. Its utility at home might be more to the point than its importance at work.

What strikes students as an essential characteristic of the technology is its flexibility. It is not just associated with the demands of work. Usefulness is, after all, what people derive from it. The application of computing for work is balanced by the utility of its value of entertainment.

> Because you can sometimes you can do your work and play games as well. I prefer to play games on them and listen to music. (Boy, year nine)

It is in the offer of constant access to light relief from a set task that makes the computer so different. It is an offer of distraction at any moment, including those times when mobile phones and i-pods are banned.

> It is not very useful all the time, they can be useful sometimes when you play games or listen to music. (Boy, year nine)

Nothing strikes the students, as they define usefulness and significance, as so characteristic as the access to a range of different sources and a host of different levels of interest. The computer is seen as a flexible machine that can offer a variety of things.

> Yeah, it is useful. You can go to the Internet. You can send things like e-mailing, playing games, things like that instead of writing. (Girl, year nine)

The variety that is appreciated is the mixture of connections, to communications as well as knowledge, to games as well as information. The computer is an alternative to drudgery, quite unlike the task of writing, which strikes students as the core of the academic experience.

"Usefulness" therefore includes a certain relief from the tedium of school. The convenience of e-mailing is partly that it can be carried out secretly and privately even in a public space, on a machine available to all. The computer cafes and airport stands exemplify the way in which the same computers give access to private and confidential messages. If the World Wide Web is a shared system, it is one which retains the individual identity of the user. This implies that it is seen as being available at any time for private use.

Even in schools, computers are approached as having the capacity to be used for personal reasons. While those who are sophisticated enough to have their own laptops can combine all kinds of personally chosen sites, even those who have to share the same computer know that it offers a means of making connections beyond itself. The question is the extent of the control and how students are prevented from making use of the potential.

If the computer offers a variety of uses, what does the school add to make it seem, in a different way, useful? If there is so much use being made of computers in a personal way, then, what is the message that school gives? There are several conflicting reactions, including the ubiquitous sense that at school the uses of computers do not seem to add anything special.

> Because you don't really learn much. (Boy, year nine)

The message that school appears to reinforce is the importance of computers for work skills. The purpose of schools is from the beginning associated by students with the preparation for employment (Cullingford 2002), and it would be surprising if any part of the curriculum were not affected in some way by this attitude. Computers are recognized as part of the preparation.

> Because like if you've got a job and you need to use a computer, that's it, really. (Girl, year nine)

> You can start your work as secretary or something. You can do so much easier looking at the database in the computer then going through so many files. It saves you time. (Girl, year nine)

The need to understand computers for the sake of the workplace contrasts with more natural pleasures that students derive from the habits of home. There is a widespread realization that, without knowledge of ICT, they will find it much harder to find employment.

> To get a good job, because most of the jobs now are to do with computers. If you don't know how to use computers, you might not get the job you want. (Girl, year nine)

> It is very important because like before, a lot of people have been ... their jobs have been cut because machines have replaced them. And that's probably what is going to happen even more now and people can control them and understand properly if they learn how to use computers. (Girl, year nine)

Students are aware of the profound effects of computers, including the replacement of many jobs. This makes their significance even greater. Students realize that they have to keep up to date, to know what is going on.

The sense that computers dominate the workplace reinforces students' awareness of their need to learn, but it also makes them feel that they do not quite know what is going on.

> It could be important because more things are becoming an electronic, whatever. I don't like it. I can't work on it properly. I don't get it. (Girl, year nine)

The necessity of keeping up, of understanding, is one of the prevailing atmospheres of school. Even when things are difficult there is an awareness that they *ought* to understand. The sense of impending significance of ICT in their futures spills over into their experiences at school.

> But it is useful for homework, because if you don't understand, you can use such place like Google and look it up. Most jobs now need basic PC skills, and it's important to have a basic knowledge. (Girl year nine)

Students recognize the importance of learning skills, not only for their homework, but for the basic preparation for jobs.

> And it's a lot easier to use and a lot quicker as well, but that depends on how good you are at using computers, and that really is basically for everything. (Boy, year nine)

> It is actually important to learn. But they don't teach you. I just talk to my friends. I don't know. (Boy, year nine)

Knowing the need to learn computing skills both for work in the future and for the more immediate demands of school does not mean it is always an easy or pleasurable experience. Another aspect of usefulness is practice. While the computer can clearly present great advantages, with the agreed caveats that this depends on the prowess of the user, some pupils still recall difficulties they have had.

> I don't know if it's useful, but it's just not for me I guess. I don't think I could use it. I mean like I come on it if I have to bit if I had to everyday? I don't like because I don't really like computers. I don't know how to do computers properly. (Girl, year nine)

"Doing" computers properly is not, of course, the same as playing games and "blogging". What at one level is taken with ease and pleasure by one student can be interpreted by another as fraught with difficulties.

> I just never been trusted with computers, because something usually bad happens. As I deleted my work two or three times then I had to do it again. (Girl, year nine)

There are a number of students, more girls than boys, who, despite understanding the significance of computers, remain shy of them. Such fear can easily lead to accidents in which work is lost. This feeds the apprehensions of the insecure.

> No I don't like ICT because I feel that when I go on to a computer I always get scared of them like if I do a click, it will delete all my work. It would be better if we just wrote on paper. I never have been really good with computers. I just don't know why. I just don't like it. I'd rather be with my friends than on computers. (Girl, year nine)

The worry about computers and the fear of them is not just a matter of unfortunate experiences but of the association with schoolwork. The academic demands of school always contrast with the social world computers also represent, the place to see friends.

For the student so much depends on the actual experience of using computers and what they are used for. They know they are important, but they also take this importance for granted. They know computers are a serious factor, but they recoil from the seriousness.

> No, it's just boring. Sometimes I like it if it is very nice work, but if it is just writing stuff and you are not working with your friends it gets kind of boring. When you are working with your friends, you can talk about all different kinds of stuff, and everyone else can give their own opinions, which makes it more enjoyable. And when you are on your own you just get bored and don't do much. Like in IT last year we made a calendar, which was very good. When you're just writing, life just typing stuff all the time he gets kind of boring. That's it, really. (Boy, year nine)

They can be no one simple attitude to computers. So much depends on the personal experiences, both at home and at school. So much depends on the way ICT is taught, whether it is part of the mechanical routine of school or whether it provides an additional excitement. So much depends on who the pupils communicate with, not just with the experience of ICT, but through it.

One important facet of computers is the facility of using them. This is a matter both of familiarity and confidence. The very shyness of using computers is an impediment. Those who take this facility for granted have a big advantage.

> I started to enjoy it more because of the work we're doing now. It was a bit boring at the beginning. I just talked and didn't pay attention. I know more than I used to so now I'm used to it. (Boy, year nine)

Computers are associated with pleasure in some circumstances and with drudgery in others. This can vary from day to day, and most students have had a range of experiences. The most central point for them, however, derives from the fact that computers are ubiquitous. They are for all kinds of purposes, and no student is unaware of what is on offer.

> I don't really like it because I like music and different kinds of music. So when I work on the computer, I feel like [sighs] I feel like listening to some music or something like that. (Boy, year nine)

The very source of pleasure can be turned into a burden.

The contrast between the pleasures and demands of computers remains. The question is how all this makes an impact on the experience of school. How is ICT presented? Is this a quite different experience for pupils?

Conclusions

Student attitudes towards computers are generally positive. This attitude, however, is not one of wonder. Students take computing for granted. They know they will be using them all their lives, for work as well as pleasure. Their positive attitudes derive from familiarity.

This sense of the ease of the familiar and the ubiquity of the equipment is somewhat undermined by school. Here, the computer is taken seriously; it is even a threat. What is produced matters, and it is significant that the fear of losing work is experienced in the conditions of school.

If the students are so positive and so familiar, what are their expectations of school? They face similar quandaries to the teachers. Are computers to be used as preparation for the world of work, to be mastered so that students will feel confident in the workplace, or are they the means through which the academic curriculum is delivered? What surprises the students is that the subject is a curious mixture of hard tasks and boredom. They might be positive about computers, but this does not mean they are positive about being taught about them. The very familiarity contrasts with the experience of school.

Chapter 6

Students' Experience of Computers

The student experience of computers at home is quite a different matter from the ethos of school. The attitudes towards using computers at school tend to be dissociated from the more general perspective of home and friends. They are, nevertheless, linked in subtle ways, and some of the small variations in opinion derive from the particulars of the home experience. The range of equipment available varies widely, as does the amounts of usage, together with the types of usage. The differences, however, lie in the very way that computers are approached and handled. If a computer is precious at home, it is because it is popular and can give whoever is using it their own form of satisfaction. If the computer is presented as precious at school, it is not just because of the paucity of the equipment, but also the earnestness with which it is regarded.

Computing is an individual experience. Schools are essentially collective. The one milieu is private – there might be many connections to many people and a plethora of communications, but it is personal. The other milieu is essentially public, where there are invariably groups of different sizes, close observation of each other and attention to the details of behaviour.

The seriousness with which computers are taken at school is as a result of several factors. One is the fact that ICT is subject to the National Curriculum and must be undertaken. Also there are strong government pressures to make teachers more skilled in using ICT generally. Another factor is that, despite the National Grid for Learning, there is not nearly enough equipment to go around.

Pupils like to work at a computer by themselves and whenever they like. They can spend hours doing this. At school, however, they treat the experience of ICT in a quite different manner. Like any other subject, it is a matter that can be tested. It will also be inspected. There are opportunities to find people wanting, of targets not met. ICT is a serious matter, not taken for granted, not simply used. It is subject to external policy decisions.

In the National Curriculum, ICT is presented in a number of ways. It is envisaged as a cross-curricular competence, but one which is both learned for its own sake and embedded in other subjects. It is supposed to enhance the learning process, whatever the subject content, and teachers are supposed to be demonstrably up-to-date and enthusiastic about it. Teachers are meant to acquire key skills in addition to all the other ones they have. Just as the National Curriculum has focused attention on the narrow core, essentially English and Mathematics, so is ICT concentrated mainly on these subjects, even if there are pressures to embody it in every part of the curriculum. There is an ambiguity in this. If computing is a generic skill, are its uses the same in French as in mathematics?

Whilst the details of policy are ambiguous, the importance of the subject is continually invoked and teachers are expected to comply. Schools are supposed to help students develop positive attitudes towards computers. Students are supposed to be competent, familiar and comfortable with technology and to learn this in school. They are also supposed to be able to stand back from the uses and reflect on the effects of ICT. If students are to be made competent, this depends on insisting that all teachers use the technology whenever possible. No teaching award is given without its including some use of ICT. If there is no other fault to find, Ofsted inspectors can always point out lapses in the use of computers. The National Curriculum insists that ICT should be used in all subjects, and by all teachers.

While the uses are supposed to be across-the-board, ICT still remains a separate subject. All the different demands and expectations cause difficulties for schools. Given the resources available and the demands, schools need to work out a way of organizing the teaching of ICT, with strict constraints on time, resources and materials. Schools have to make choices, for instance about whether to take into account the students' previous knowledge. They have to work out whether to rely on the prevailing classroom organization or on the availability of computers, in large or in small groups.

Certain basic patterns of provision were followed by all the schools. They devoted a double period per week (one and a half hours) in the timetable to ICT. This tended to be divided between teaching and providing experiences for the students in the hope that they would practice and develop the skills that had been demonstrated.

The schools adopted three modes of timetabling ICT. The first was the introduction of the subject in its own right; the second was the teaching of computer studies, as if this were a skill to be developed, rather than a subject; and the third was to develop ICT across the curriculum, to try to embed it (and embed learning about computers) within subjects. There was naturally a significant amount of overlap, and to some extent there was a natural progression from one mode to another. The students were constantly acquiring new skills and learning how to use these skills within different parts of the curriculum. They were also making more use of ICT in their own way, as in the presentation of their work. To some extent this was a natural, if disregarded, overlap between the skills learned at home and those applied at school.

One of the distinctive features of ICT provision is the fact that, because of its ambiguous status – both a subject and a provision of other subjects – it does not have a separate identity within a department. Most of the schools had an ICT coordinator, whose function was not only to lead the subject teaching but also to liaise with all the other departments. Some had considerable autonomy and responsibility, but in one school there was no designated ICT teacher at all. The task of coordinating the uses of computers was taken up by a technician.

The differences in provision were marked. The six schools all had a combination of different makes and types of computer and one had Acorn machines, a nostalgic note. The number of computers provided had a clear effect on the kind of teaching, both in terms of separate rooms and the ratio of students to computers. Two pupils would often have to share the same computer; in other schools they would work by themselves. Some schools eased the burden on lessons by giving access during lunch hours and after school. Many classrooms had a few computers scattered around as well as dedicated rooms. The impression is of schools doing their best to cope, trying to deal with a difficult situation.

Three of the schools taught ICT as a specialist subject and assessed pupils through an RSA scheme, concentrating on the basic skills of word-processing, spreadsheets, databases and PowerPoint. There was a feeling among the staff and students that these things could be useful not only for their own sake but in developing other subjects. They were clearly found useful in terms of homework. The degree to which these skills were transferred to the other subjects is open to question.

If there were differences in approach and provision, there were also separate approaches to the way the teaching of ICT was organized. The most common practice was to set exercises for students to carry out, with one following on from another. The students usually had their work printed out so that they could assess themselves and be assessed once they had finished the task. The consistent assumption was that there was a hierarchy of skills and knowledge that a student would acquire stage by stage, progressing from one level to another. This gave a point to all the assessments, a kind of behavioural checklist of achievement.

One reason for the constant exercises was the combination of large classes, individuals working by themselves and the shortage of time. The mean number of hours allocated to the teaching of computing was 1.53 hours per week. The majority of the students reported that they would work on the computers for one hour per week, but this factor was changed overall by the third of the students who said that they worked on computers for two hours per week and the minority who said they worked on them far longer. What was striking was that boys reported working far longer with computers than girls, the average times being between 2.9 hours per week for boys and 1.37 hours per week for girls.

What was clear, and clearly common practice, was the way that the computer lessons were based on the passive reception of ideas, and the constant practice and testing of the exercises. The tradition of rote learning seemed to prevail, reinforced by the attitudes expressed in one teacher's command to "only do what you are told to". As another teacher, in her defence, explained to her class: "There is only one of me and about 32 of you. So please be quiet and just let me finish what I have to do and then go and practice". Many students had booklets given to them that contained a series of routine exercises, the techniques of word-processing, which depended on constant repetition until it became familiar and could be applied to other skills.

Such practices depend on spending time on the keyboard. This is not something that can be a shared activity. While group work can be used in a purposeful way, the regime of schooling, with its tests and examinations, fosters the cult of the individual in competition with others. While there is a great deal of complex learning that can take place in group discussions, groups are usually a means of organizing resources (Galton and Williamson 1992). Such a focus on resources means that, instead of individual work, the experience of most pupils was working in pairs, which demanded a certain amount of patience. Most of the schools did their best to find time for individual practice, timetabling the precious resources carefully.

Nevertheless, the sight of two students at the same computer was the norm. When they shared the computer they had to negotiate their own time on the keyboard. Sometimes they stored their work on the same disk; sometimes they had their own. It was remarkable how well the students dealt with the necessity of working with each other. They not only displayed patience and encouraged each other by sharing ideas, helping with decisions and talking generally, but they also helped other pupils at different workstations.

Of course there were difficulties. The pace at which individuals wanted to work varied greatly. It was common to see one group of students finish a set of tasks very quickly, while another cohort had not finished by the end of the allocated time, so that they would do it later, either in free time or the following week.

The students expressed their preference to work by themselves, but were forgiving of the circumstances. "Although I prefer to work alone, I did not mind at all". By working in some pairs where they could not help each other, certain students were clearly making no headway. Because they did not want to be thought "dumb" they hid their ignorance, and remained as invisible as possible. Even if the teachers encouraged each student to ask for clarification, there were those who preferred to remain quiet. When cooperation was planned, students communicated well and were helpful and accommodating. Most of the work that was undertaken in pairs was, however, set as an individual task. This meant that the spirit of competition was never far away.

The instructions that teachers gave were either written up on the board or on the overhead projector or given out as exercise booklets or sheets. The students were expected to finish each task before going onto the next one. Such drills meant that the students were expected to be able to handle information, to store it and retrieve it. They were supposed to be able to use PowerPoint and create presentations. They were also encouraged to illustrate findings with pictures, graphics and charts. What they were learning were the skills in using the computer, not using it as a source of knowledge or exploration but as a means of presentation.

The ability to develop such skills showed in the way that homework was prepared. The sense of difference between the individual work that could be carried out at home and the social contexts appropriate in school was clear. The work of assessment was increasingly prepared entirely at home; school was the place where it was handled in. Thus the knowledge of how to use a computer to generate material was learned because of the demands of school. At home, the students were not just playing games, but demonstrating their awareness of the need to refine the appearance of the work they were handing in, as well as knowing where to find information.

In terms of basic confidence in the use of computers, it was clear that the very familiarity with which the students accepted computing at home, when they possessed the equipment, was subtly undermined when they were in school. Computing was no longer an aspect of domesticity, but a different kind of challenge. It had to be taken seriously.

The sense of discomfiture that a significant number of students felt was because the circumstances were so different and so changeable. They sometimes had computers in the classroom, sometimes with dedicated spaces. They were not only working as individuals, but also sometimes in pairs or in groups. The work that was presented to them was often in the form of set tasks they had to carry out. On other occasions, lessons were presented in a more individual manner. The previous knowledge students brought with them made little difference to what was presented to them. The experience they received of the school, from the presentation of the curriculum to the uses of the equipment, was not only more formal but also more piecemeal.

One problem for the students and the teachers was the conflicting demands of ICT. Computers were envisaged as a significant resource, a powerful aid to learning. At the same time, ICT was a formal subject that had to be learned for its own sake. The significance of particular skills for future employability was highlighted, and yet many of these skills were, in themselves, simply a means to gain access to more knowledge. All the time there was a sense of a different future, with laptops for each individual and direct involvement of the secondary sources, but this vision was mitigated by the standard procedures of school and the demands of the National Curriculum. The central dilemma is whether the students were being taught to use computers or using computers for the sake of learning.

Conclusions

The ways in which the teaching of ICT was approached varied greatly between the schools. This suggests the difficulties and ambiguities that surround the introduction of computers because the theory that should support the subject has never been thought through.

More pointed still were the contrasts and conflicts of approach even within the same school. Practice varied, not out of a desire for variety, but because there seemed little coherence in the attitudes and expectations of the subject. But then, there is the outstanding question of whether computing is a subject at all.

The students felt the confusion. They realized that there would be complex attitudes, but they also felt that these were due to incoherence, not in the individual teachers, who were doing their best, but in the contradictory expectations of schools. Computers were presented to them as a subject, but also as a skill to be learned. They were also taken to be a means to an end, although what this end was remained unclear.

Above all, the students were aware of the contrast between two types of experience. One was a style of learning and communicating that was personal, individual and exploratory. The other was the sense of imposition and control.

Chapter 7
The Uses of ICT in Schools

For many years we have listened to one big prediction and another great exhortation. The general prediction comes from anyone involved with policy. The most long-standing exhortation, which sometimes sounds like a plea, is to make the new technology so central that the whole nature of schooling will be changed. Just as there have been predictions of changes in job patterns, with offices disappearing while people work at home, so we have been urged to reconsider what might happen when all the power of microtechnology is brought into play in schools.

The exhortation, aimed at teachers, is for them to make every possible use of the available technology, to consider various programs and new devices that are to transform all styles of teaching and learning. All awards for outstanding teachers are directed at those who avail themselves of the new technology and teacher educators are clearly instructed to ascertain that their students are wedded to the use of computers. It is not only an extra but seen as a vital means of delivering the set curriculum.

These exhortations are understandable. There is no doubt about the transformational possibilities, even if these have not been thought through. Long after the popularity of Marshall McLuhan, the changes to communication and to styles of communicating, to the storage of and access to materials, have been noted in a variety of ways. The problem is that the assumption about the rise of new technologies is faced with the reality of an education system. The predictions imply that schools will disappear in the form in which we know them and that the students will work individually at home. Many of the commentaries have implied that the teacher is redundant.

In the same period that such predictions have been so easily made, the educational system as a whole has gone in the opposite direction. The attempts to open up the curriculum and to involve parents, to experiment with teaching styles and to liberalize the governance of schools have been replaced by a centralized control, the insistence on traditional models of teaching, on targets and tests, and a curriculum weighed down and intent upon detail. All teachers experience this. The paperwork, the extra demands and the scrutiny of what they are doing mean that, while the instinct to experiment may be the same as ever, their chances of doing so are diminished. Teachers are caught between the potential of ICT and the demands of the National Curriculum.

The individual experiments with new teaching approaches, based on the belief that students' learning can be enhanced, continue unabated. The enthusiasm to take up what ICT offers is unabated, but it must be acknowledged that the education system remains implacable. Individual endeavour is diminished by the more general ethos of schools. The very excitement of new opportunities is subtly undermined by the well-documented, centralized control (Elliott 1998).

The strategies for the introduction and development of ICT have not been thought through. They were an addition to an already burdened curriculum rather than a replacement. They have been formalized when they could have been a genuine alternative. Above all, ICT has been seen as a subject in its own right rather than as a means to an end: a skill to be learned, rather than an opportunity for independent learning. Above all, the lack of a genuine and practical vision for ICT has meant that teachers have been confronted by having to use the technology and also to teach it. The development of computer studies has been paralleled by, and has undermined, the encouragement to use the technology in different subjects.

That computers are a central part of the school experience is not in doubt. Even if the provision of resources varies, no school is without the means of making use of ICT in a variety of ways. The many books that introduce ideas of how to create effective teaching strategies for ICT demonstrate how seriously the subject is taken. Students' lives are supposed to be transformed by the experience and the whole feeling of learning fundamentally altered.

All students undertake computer studies in some form. They take it for granted that this is a necessity. It does not mean that they anticipate that there will be anything particularly exciting in store. The pleasures of using computers are associated with the home, with free access to the Internet and with the materials that are available online. At school, the emphasis is much more on the skills themselves, rather than the reasons why the skills are learned in the first place.

The underlying justification for emphasizing the ability to manipulate programs and produce data sheets and PowerPoint presentations is future employability. To a large extent this is the whole purpose of school, from the students' point of view (Cullingford 2002). From an early age, they understand that they have to go through this rite of passage with the ultimate goal being their marketability for employment, whether through higher qualifications or through a chosen vocation. All subjects, not only English and mathematics, are seen in the light of this purpose, since they are told of no other. ICT falls into the category of a subject that is emphasized for its utility, for the skills involved like the decoding of script or the techniques of numeracy.

There is always a tension between the acquisition of specific skills and the purposes for which they are learned, as in the learning of synthetic phonics and the pleasure or utility of reading a book. Computer skills might be emphasized in the curriculum, but they are more instinctively applied at home, and sometimes within other lessons.

Whatever the socio-economic status of the school, and whatever the contrasts of resources, all students stated that they did use computers in school. The number of computers in each school ranged from 90 to 278. The students in years nine and ten had a weekly opportunity, for about an hour, to use the computers. As there are constant and significant changes being made to computers – laptops being an example to which we will return – the schools often had to make do with relatively old equipment. This put the emphasis on the skills of computing, rather than their uses.

The types of computers used at school were mostly PCs. Some 80% of the students said that they were using them. The other students were divided between those who used Macintosh computers and those who used Acorns. Some of the older computers could not be connected online. Some were not very powerful, and many students could not get access to the most recent information. The quality of the machines, and the quality of experience, varied a great deal.

The time spent with a computer, which is generally limited, can be so much more valuable if equipment is up to date. The National Grid for Learning was a commitment to provide not only better resources, but also to emphasize the importance of the Internet in provideing access to, and sharing, greater amounts of knowledge. The experience of the students, however, remained fairly unsophisticated, at least in school.

In modifying the National Curriculum (Department for Education 1995), the government stated that at key stage three students should be taught to become critical, and largely autonomous, users of information technology. They were to understand the limitations as well as the strengths of the tools and the results they produced. Schools were not given advice on any particular form of organization, but were encouraged to apply ICT broadly across the curriculum. This focuses attention on the choices schools face in providing specific computer awareness courses for teachers as well as pupils, which would allow subject teachers to assume a basic prior knowledge in encouraging the using of ICT within subjects themselves. The idea is that the skills would be developed alongside their application. Many schools operated a mixture of the approaches, which meant that the student experiences were varied and they were unaware of the overall strategy.

In the most limited experiences of ICT, students were instructed by a technician and engaged in learning basic skills to prepare computer materials. In these cases, computers were not used for academic purposes. There were instances in some schools where old computers were used solely for recreational purposes with a minimum of trained ICT supervision. The different uses of computers in school depended on the number of machines available, the time devoted to the subject, the expertise of the teacher, the quality of the software and course materials as well as the students' prior experience and their motivation.

One of the most significant variables in the experience of computers is the time allocated to their use. If computers are to make an impact as a learning resource, it would be expected that they would make up a substantial part of the school day. This would enable individual learning to take place with access to high-quality material, and the acquisition of the ability to explore and organize a number of different subjects.

All the students had experienced using a computer. Nearly half of them said that the time they were allocated was about one hour per week. This is very little time, surprisingly little given the amount of emphasis not only on computing skills, but on the great gain to be derived from access to the Internet. The mean number of hours per week for all the students was just under two. The longest amount of time that the students reported using computers in school was five hours per week. Whilst this was much more true of boys than girls, it was also only a small minority of them.

Overall, there was little gender difference in the time spent using a computer. Whilst nearly 50% used the computer for one hour per week, 30% used it for two hours and 11% for three hours. This makes ICT a marginal part of the experience of being in school. It makes it clear to the students that is not something embedded within the curriculum or a seamless part of the learning. The limited amount of time suggests that computers are not central to the learning of different subjects, although, as we will note, there are attempts to spread its use.

If computers are a limited part of the school week, let alone day, there is no surprise if the emphasis is on the skills of using a computer. It is difficult to reconcile a widespread application of the technology and the small amount of time devoted to it. It could be argued that such a limitation makes ICT a precious quality, something to be prized and cherished. This is not, however, the way in which most students experience computers at home when the time passes by so easily.

There has been a long tradition of introducing computers as a discrete package in which, over several years, students received one hour of lessons in computer-aided design, word-processing, the computer as a learning aid, computer models, electronic music and databases (Wellington 1988). Given the constraints of time, this kind of program would normally be deemed the most appropriate. Over the years the development of ICT has been largely as a separate subject for this reason. Three-quarters of the students reported that they studied ICT as a distinct subject, mostly in one lesson per week. The National Curriculum, through its statutory orders, named ten foundation subjects. These did not include ICT. ICT was regarded, like health education, as a "theme" rather than a subject. Later, five cross-curricular themes were also added, such as economic and industrial understanding and citizenship. The use of information technology, "which could be taught through other subjects" (ibid., p. 88) was then divided into two components, information technology and design and technology.

One might wonder if the advice about the curriculum, the subjects and the themes amounts to a coherent whole. The introduction of a new statutory order, like careers education guidance, does not mean a reduction in the demands on any other subject. The limitation of time affects everything. It is no surprise if schools concentrate their resources on dealing with ICT as a separate issue. At the same time, they are constantly cajoled into applying computers across the whole of the curriculum.

For three-quarters of the students, ICT was experienced as a separate subject. Of these, two-thirds had one lesson per week and about 10% two lessons. This leaves a quarter of the students who said that they had no ICT lessons as such. This might not be a reflection of the official timetable, but it was the perception of the students. They felt that the school experience of using computers had passed them by. On the other hand, they might have thought that the study of ICT for its own sake was not the point. They came across computing as something using other parts of the curriculum for the purposes of access to knowledge. The 25% of students who did not experience ICT as a separate subject could still use computing in a variety of ways, on their own or embedded with other experiences.

The expectation that schools would make use of computing throughout the curriculum has been difficult to meet, but these students show that the theme of ICT does, indeed, insinuate itself into other subjects. The use might be uneven and occasional, but their awareness of ICT was not dependent entirely on the formal lessons. Some 90% of the students made use of computers in subjects other than ICT. In a variety of subjects there was some kind of access to work stored on computers. Although this might be the most natural use of the facility, it is a very different experience from the formal skills on which they could be tested.

The amount of time that students used computers outside the formal lessons varied. Some had no other experience than the formal lessons, but a third had at least some time, up to an hour, in which ICT was applied. There were a few pupils, more boys than girls, who made use of computers outside the formal lessons. This could be in a variety of ways, including private access at lunch and other breaks or after school. So the experience of ICT was not all formal. For a significant number of students, the use of computers could be fitted into a number of opportunities, mostly short, but more individual.

The periods of time that the students report show the difference between perceived and actual time. This is not because it might vary from week to week, but because the definitions of using a computer in itself are as flexible and as capricious as "time on task". When students are sitting in a lesson, how much of the time are they actually working rather than gathering materials, whispering to friends or waiting for something to happen? When they are ostensibly working as a task, how much of the time are they concentrating rather than daydreaming? There are few moments when complete concentration remains sustained. Sitting by a computer is no different in that there are two sources of distraction. One is other people, those who are also waiting their turn or for instruction. The other is the computer itself, for its multiple layers of information. How much time is spent on the computer is a difficult figure to measure. Time can pass quickly or slowly depending entirely on the task and the involvement in it.

The desire to integrate ICT with other subjects has been a long-standing and essential part of the initial vision of what computers could do. The reason for the concentration on skills was partly due to the poverty of resources. The potential of ICT in other subjects has long been established (Cox 1993). The students who made regular use of information technology could achieve better results in English, mathematics, science and geography. They were not only interested in having access to information, but also developed their reasoning skills. The assumption has also long been held that computers will pervade the whole of the curriculum (Bork 1985).

The students were asked whether they had any experience of this use of computing, of its integration with other subjects. This was, after all, the policy. In

English 60% of the student had used computers. This was mainly for writing essays and stories and would have enhanced their confidence in presenting material. In mathematics 55% of the students had been engaged with computing, rather more boys than girls. Whilst there were a number of programs in mathematics these were still a small part of their experience. Computer instruction in mathematics can be beneficial (Reglin 1990). It has not yet, however, become the main or preferred mode for instruction.

Nevertheless, there were signs that in the two dominating subjects some use was being made of computers, even if only at the level of word-processing. What then of science, a subject that should lend itself to ICT? There is a range of software that has been developed to enhance and stimulate the learning of the sciences. It is possible to learn about the most up-to-date work on the Internet and pick up facts and pictures from reference sources. It is also possible to develop models and employ model-building software and readings using data loggers (Mumtaz 2000). Some 20% of the students reported having used computers in lessons in chemistry, physics and biology, a larger number of boys than girls.

This lack of extensive use of a valuable resource is disappointing; one would have thought after earlier efforts that the numbers of students involved in computing would be higher (Logan 1988). The question is whether all the creative and interesting programs that are available fit into the demands of the National Curriculum. The syllabus still has to be covered and the tests prepared for. Many of the most interesting scientific programs are not directly about the facts that are supposed to be learned. As in the early days of the Open University, it was programs that were not directly related to the syllabus that proved most interesting and memorable. Emphasis on practical scientific skills in government directives might also have diminished the use of the material available online. Just as there is little use of educational technology in countries with a powerful central curriculum, for want of time, or for fear of students not meeting the requirements of testing, so the emphasis on targets could be diminishing the uses of ICT in scientific subjects.

If computers are not being used in the mainstream subjects, the core curriculum, what then of subjects like design technology or business studies? It is difficult to imagine either subject not being fully integrated with ICT. All kinds of technology, including graphics, are dependent on computer programs. No business can function without computers, whether for counting, communicating or in robotics. When the National Curriculum was first debated, all subjects had their proponents who advocated making theirs the central subject, around which the others would find their place. The most vociferous advocacy was perhaps for technology, whether this was the core into which everything else would fit or a subject that would permeate all others (Boulter 1989).

Half the students reported making use of ICT in design technology. Whilst this might seem satisfactory, it is at an odd variance to practixe in the world of work, whatever the nature of the design. Similarly, while one would expect business studies to be naturally dominated by computing, only 20% of the students said that they used computers in this subject. This is the same percentage of pupils who said that they use computers in the specialist design technology subjects of textiles and food.

In the material regularly produced by the Department of Education (in all its various changes of nomenclature), there is nearly always a strong argument about the value of using computers in subjects like geography and history. The ability to access and evaluate historical, social and economic information from various sources, and the power to create simulations and measure phenomena, demonstrate the potential of using such a powerful tool, not just for access but also as a means of manipulating data.

About a third of the students had used computers in history. About a quarter had used computers in geography, and in religious education. The ambitious intent has not been met by a commensurate upsurge in the actual use of computers. This has, for all kinds of reasons, been piecemeal. The amount of time devoted to computing is small, and while it is spread amongst different subjects, there appears to be no concerted strategy in which computers are a central means of delivering the curriculum for reasons to do with lack of resources and the demands of the tests.

Nevertheless, computers are seen, even if this is only an occasional glimpse, in different parts of the curriculum. About a quarter of the students have made use of the technology in art and music. In one subject, where computer programs can be used to support the skills of repetitive learning, there is a much higher incidence of computer use. This is in modern languages, when nearly half the students taking the subject find themselves using computers.

When the pupils spoke about their experience of ICT at school certain themes emerged. One was the lack of time devoted to computers, overall, whether as a separate subject or embedded in others.

> You just do it once a week, which is not very good. You should learn more, not just once a week. You could forget what you have learned. But if it's every day or every couple of days you could have learnt more about IT. (Boy, year nine)

> I don't think it's good enough of me really, because I'm doing GCSE. I need to know more about it really. (Girl, year 10)

The sense of the importance of ICT is not matched by the amount of time devoted to it. It has to compete with other subjects, and they in their turn are constrained by the demands of the curriculum. It is telling that there is no overall shift to the programs offered in all subjects through ICT.

The students are aware from their personal experience of what any search engine can offer. They know that they can juggle various sources of information, but this does not happen in the constraints of school. It is as if the material available through computers is not to be taken too seriously.

Sometimes if we are doing something that we really can't get in books. Then you can go into the IT room, but most of the time we use books, and look in the library for stuff like that. (Boy, year nine).

It is as if the Internet were a last resort, or the information it presented could not be controlled and was therefore under suspicion. Students remained aware of the Internet, and yet were made to pretend that they were generally ignorant.

But sometimes we use the Internet. Like once at the end of the term in school. (Boy, year nine).

If computers might have entered into the students' daily lives, they do not figure as central to the experience of school.

Oh, we just use it in one lesson every week. You just use it in IT. You don't get it in other lessons which could help you. Because you should go to the Internet and find out other things, like equipment. You could order stuff on it, but you can't. You have to learn what the ICT teacher says, and you have to do it. That's it really. (Boy, year nine)

The constraints are not just those of time but of following a clear sense of instructions. The possibilities of personal initiatives are ignored.

But we don't use them in other subjects as much. Sometimes we use them in maths. (Girl, year nine)

Whatever the circumstances, the experience of using computers is not a major one. It is limited by a number of impediments, making way for other more pressing matters.

It's not computing to study it as a separate subject. Sometimes we use it in other subjects. That's if the teachers booked us into the computer room. (Boy, year nine)

All the time students demonstrate the peculiarity of ICT in its position as both a separate subject and a pervasive means to an end. It has its own dedicated space, and it is supposed to be embedded in all the classrooms. This lack of focus leads to a certain undermining of confidence. There seems little excitement afforded by ICT.

We do IT as a separate subject, but it's really boring. Like we use the Internet and it's really slow. And you are not allowed to go on to the game websites. They are blocked and stuff like that. (Boy, year nine)

We don't have it as a separate subject. But if you want to pick it up as a separate subject then you can pick it up this year, and you study it next year. That is all but I don't think is very important to pick it as a separate subject. (Girl, year nine)

Conclusions

The central dilemma is perfectly clear to the students. The subject of ICT, taught formally and separately, is different from the usual uses of computers, which are at the service of other matters. Given the students' experience of computing in the home, one wonders if computers can ever be a natural part of school life, schools being the way they are.

The irony is that the National Curriculum was introduced at a time when computers were beginning to make an impact. The Education Reform Act could not contrast more with the flexibility and individuality of learning from computers. It imposed rigid and detailed content in all subjects, with levels, tests, targets and key stages. It presented a series of inflexible demands just at the time when computers were being envisioned as freeing people from the rigidities of formal learning.

The contrast between the experience of computers at home and school is highlighted by the fact that the amount of time devoted to them in school is very small. There are many reasons for this, but the effects are clear. What strikes the students most of all is the unimaginative ways in which computers are presented. Teachers suffer all kinds of constraints; the ways in which schools operate are at odds with the rest of students' experiences.

Chapter 8
How ICT is Taught

The initial excitement with new technology is directed at its potential, at the way it was supposed to operate. However, new technology can still be approached with a certain amount of apprehension and suspicion, as well as interest. There is a growing concern with its more subtle and pervasive effects, as happened with the introduction of television. After a time, a new technology is taken for granted, made use of, as it becomes so much a normal part of life that it blends seamlessly into the everyday, even if it does not become invisible. It is then that a real concern with the effects should be encouraged, but this is rarely done.

Like other technologies, ICT causes all kinds of reactions, and this needs to be understood in order to explore the experience of pupils. The differences in attitudes to the uses of computers at home and in school is already clear. This exacerbates the distinction between how an instrument that is treated as entertainment and utility in one environment is approached as something that is to be taken very seriously in another. Anything associated with school will anyway be assumed to have an earnest intent, but this is made more emphatic because of the divide between ICT as a subject in its own right and as an instrument of support and transaction in other subjects.

ICT is, in one sense, another teaching aid. Like overhead projectors, videos and white boards, it can enhance the learning process. It can make lessons far more interesting. On the other hand, it takes time both to set up and to learn how to use it, time which teachers, struggling to keep up with the National Curriculum, have difficulty mustering. Wherever there is a strong syllabus that must be taught and which will be tested, there is pressure on teachers to ignore technologies, however attractive they may be. While the most obvious excuse for routine lessons is not having enough equipment available, the real reason is often the pressure of time (Al-Qudah 2002).

There are many extra resources available to support teaching, not only in terms of equipment but also in terms of content. The possibilities of access are great, but there are always difficulties in making use of it, in planning, in being aware of what is available. After all, the curriculum has its own momentum, which inhibits straying from its path. The time for suddenly having an idea, and following it, or seizing the opportunity, those lessons so much relished in the past, is much reduced. There is so much the teacher has to cover.

How then do teachers in ICT lessons and in others actually present the new technologies? Already, we detect a dichotomy between the use of teaching aids to deliver the curriculum most effectively, and the stress on the teaching aid itself. Computers are not simply there to support the teacher. They are not primarily aids or extras, as one could define television programs. Computers are approached as instruments that need to be mastered.

There are many experts who give advice on using computers as well as on programming. Apart from all the huge manuals, there is no doubt that it has long been felt that there is a lot to be learned. The question is whether it is best to learn about using the computer through access to it, or by being instructed. There is a growing trend towards making the instructions and options available on the computer itself. This emphasizes learning through use, rather than the preparation of a skill. One can draw an analogy with learning to read. Those who are most skilled at reading have learned extensively by themselves, by decoding, by detecting the purpose of reading and wanting to do it. This is dependent on others only in that such learning depends on the provision of books, on being told stories, on sharing picture books and on following the techniques and developing an awareness of the pleasure to be derived. Against this, the educational emphasis on reading is that of skills, of synthetic phonics, of graphemes and phonemes, on direction rather than support. The point is that the emphasis needs to be on helping the pupil to learn, ostensibly for him or herself.

As with the teaching of reading, the educational system is concerned with instruction, with the convening of distinct skills. This implies that pupils receive instructions about the way they should use computers. While there is always supposed to be an individual relationship between the computer and its user, this is mediated in school by an instructor. The students were asked if they were taught computing through the use of instructions before they started work on them in the school; 97% confirmed that they did.

Even with computers, however many there are available, the teaching mode of giving instructions at the start of the lessons continues. Some 43% of the students reported that they always began every lesson with a series of instructions, so that each lesson had a separate and complete plan. In all, 37% said that they were frequently given instructions before starting, and another 17% that they were sometimes given preliminary instructions. This was clearly a continuation of the traditional mode of delivery of having an expert with the knowledge of the manual, passing on what is learned to others. Computers can themselves demonstrate and deliver instructions, but this is not the preferred mode (Morton 1996). While ICT suggests the use of inferential reasoning, and the monitoring and regulation of problem-solving, these are sidelined in favour of more traditional presentations of facts (Butterfield and Nelson 1989). Meta-cognitive skills appear to be replaced by old-fashioned techniques of transfer.

Instructions given by teachers can vary. They do not have to be a verbal introduction, although it is worth pointing out that the key was not so much the mode as the fact that the lesson would begin with the teacher. Computer use had to wait until the teacher had finished. The students were asked what kind of instructions they were given by the teacher. While more than one type could be used, more than two-thirds of the students said that there was a predominance of two types of instruction. The teacher would naturally give verbal instructions, but would also write on the board. Indeed, "writing on the board" was the most frequently cited means of instruction. The students also mentioned the use of handouts for them to look at before going to the computers. One minor variant to the blackboard was the use of the overhead projector.

What is clear is that the means of approaching the use of computers was mostly traditional, as if computing was another subject to be added to the curriculum and tested. The mode of whole class instruction remained central. While one-third of the students also cited learning through the instruction sheet on the computer screen, the significance of whole class teaching remained. There was the same task for all. Far from going their individual ways, the students remained focused on one matter at a time, presumably going at the same pace. It is as if the theories of individualized learning, in which through an act of "bricolage" many different levels and ways of accumulating ideas from a variety of sources can take place, were put in contrast to the traditional modes of learning. For some, the notion of "bricolage", an eclectic gathering of sources of knowledge, and the mixing up of different levels of interest, from the trivial to the weighty, is central to the understanding of the use of computers (Cuthell 1999).

The ways in which people can manipulate knowledge and have almost instant access to a range of different types of material should make learning from computers quite different. Juggling with different items on the same screen, keeping in touch with friends, other news and the set tasks all at the same time makes the process of looking at information different. And yet the experience of the classroom remains the same. While the availability of computers increases, the instruction methods do not change (Gbomita 1997). The implications of ICT do not appear to have been understood, let alone embraced (Morton 1996).

The students were accustomed to the tradition of receiving information. The interactivity and the iterative possibilities of the computers themselves were a marked contrast to the traditional forms of lessons. In one state, the students are in an anonymous group; in the other they have their own dialogue and their own control. Teachers, however, know that, despite the impediments of class size, the most successful methods are those that manage to engage individual attention. Pupils long for an intellectual relationship with a teacher (Cullingford 2002). The fact that few manage to attain this is not just because of class sizes; it is because many have given up trying (Pye 1989). Interactivity is central to the expectations of both teachers and learners (Yacci 2000).

Students were asked what kind of instruction the teachers employed during the class as well as before it. One might have surmised that with pupils working on computers there would be many opportunities for individual attention. Rather more than a quarter said that the teachers gave individual instructions during the class. About 10% said that they were instructed in small groups and slightly fewer that they were placed in larger groups, where the teacher could deal with them. Half the students pointed out that the teacher would respond if they needed help. In addition to these more personal interactions, however, the students were conscious of the fact that general instructions continued. Some 93% of them said that teachers gave instructions to the whole class, not just at the beginning of the lesson, but throughout it. This puts the central relationship not with the computer, but between the teacher and the whole class. The students reported that they were told. "Do whatever you were told to do and follow the instructions on the instructions sheet".

A lot depends on the number of computers available, a fact that lap tops could do much to address, but much also depends on the ways in which the computers are used. They can be like a surrogate teacher, or at least a type of teaching assistant. They can help with the enhancement of the central curriculum. The design of computer assisted learning is based on interactive software, and the ability to adapt to different styles of learning. The theory is that CAL "will" (it is nearly always in the future) transform the learning environment. The arguments for such learning are many for they reiterate the chance to raise standards, as well as motivation, not only to engage the students but also increase their thinking skills.

While the computer is normally worked at individually, it can also enhance collaborative learning, used as a tool that focuses discussion by groups (Squires et al. 2000). Instructions were normally given to the group as a whole, but they could involve groups of different sizes, especially if there was a task in which discussion would be necessary. In traditional classes there has always been an essential mixture of general classroom talk and organization, with closed questions to which the answer is either right or wrong, and the individual is engaged in silent work. This has not changed, even with the advent of computers, but there have also been many different uses of groups (Galton and Williamson 1995). Given the flexibility of computers, the possibilities are many.

When the students were asked about their classroom experiences, they demonstrated the difference between the introductory period when instructions were given out and what followed afterwards. They were asked to say how they used computers at school, which was taken by them as being in the classroom. Some 11% said that they continued to use computers as a class. Slightly fewer pointed out that they were working by themselves but would ask for help if they needed it. This contrasts with the 87% who asserted that they worked individually. For them, the instructions were soon over, and afterwards they were expected to get on with things by themselves.

A quarter of the students said that they worked in small groups, but the general experience was of a contrast between general instructions and the carrying out of the instructions as individuals. Some pupils worked in pairs, but this was probably because there were not enough computers to do anything but share. The potential of students working together is often recognized, not least by the students themselves, although they were also aware that there were temptations in the pleasure of talking to their friends, and that they were essentially on their own.

Working as individuals might seem the traditional way to spend the majority of time in the classroom. However, this does not mean that it is full of routines and exercises. Working on a computer is an individual matter. The students were, therefore, asked how they preferred to use computers in school, whether they appreciated the opportunity to work with others in groups or in the class as a whole. Three-quarters were adamant that they liked to work by themselves. This appeared to them to be the most appropriate way of handling computers, and certainly the one to which they were most accustomed. Of the others who preferred not to work by themselves, the most popular mode of learning was being in a pair, where they could talk to each other.

The fact that students prefered to work individually with computers could be the result of what they were accustomed to do at home, not just to engage with the computer without interruption, but to do so in the way they preferred. The world that is opened up by the Internet is one which is packed with contacts and with information but it is also a private one. A slightly different question was put to them as to which method they thought they had used best to learn most. They were asked specifically if they could get more out of the experience if they worked by themselves or in various kinds of group. The answers to this question were virtually identical to the last. Not only did they prefer working individually, but they also thought this was most effective.

Given the iterative nature of many computer programs, it is not surprising that pupils preferred to work individually. In other lessons there were not the same strong beliefs expressed about working or being by themselves. Individual work in most lessons is associated with routines and with repetitions of previous work, "with time on-task", with having to get things done and with copying things out. The alternative is seen as the pleasure of talking with other students, with friends about their ideas and opportunities to discuss as well as carry out activities. Computing is a different matter to them.

There are many activities that can be carried out using a computer, the most obvious one being word-processing for a variety of purposes. While there are programs that can be acquired, like BASIC or PASCAL, and computer applications in various subjects, the routines of computing lie in access to, and communicating, information. Computer awareness courses cover information handling and stock control as well as word-processing. Students can learn spreadsheets and databases, but the most frequent activity remains word-processing (Mumtaz 2000).

The students were asked what they used computers for in school. Some 88% said that it was for word processing, but there were several other activities they carried out as well: 73% said that they created spreadsheets; 70% used computers for the Internet; 45% said that they used computers both for making databases and for PowerPoint. About a third said that they would use computers for drawing pictures and a similar proportion said that they used computers in school for e-mail. E-mail was associated with home use rather than with school. It is an essential and growing communication system. While school was seen as a social centre and as a physical meeting place, socializing with a large group of friends through e-mail tended to be an activity of the home.

The development of interactive web-based instruction suggests that pupils could gain more knowledge and information from individual work with the computer. There are web sites and encyclopaedias that contain far more information than any single teacher can provide. However, did the students see the computer as the most important source? How did they compare the information they acquired with other means like books and teachers? Was the computer now the central source of knowledge? When asked if the computer could give them access to more or less information than other sources, just under half said it was the same. It was comparable to other means of knowledge. Yet more than half asserted that it could give more information, or even much more information. Just 1% found that other sources of knowledge were more efficient.

There was no question in students' minds about the power of the computer. For them, it is the most vital source of information, more than the library the textbooks and the teacher. This puts a premium on the individual, knowing how to gain access to the material. At the same time the computer is used as much as a substitute for pen and paper as for anything else. It is a means of presentation, of preparing material, correcting it and polishing it. Drafting on screen, because it is so flexible, is a different matter than drafting ideas on the page. Whether it is better remains a moot point, but it certainly allows for more guessing, all restructuring and more experimentation. The fact that matters can also be stored and recycled or used in different places, suggests that the ways of thinking associated with producing text are changed with the different medium. Whether it "involves the suppression of the unconscious and our sense of self" (Beynon 1992, p. 180) is doubtful, but that it is different, even from the most pragmatic point of view advantageous, is certain.

If computers are an alternative means of access to information to traditional sources from books and handouts to teachers, is it also one that is easier to use? Given all the lessons on computing skills, one might have thought the subject to be complex and demanding. The students were asked whether they found using a computer easier than worksheets or books to perform a task. Only 2% found it more difficult. While 15% found it on a par with other offerings, 82% found that using a computer was easy or very easy. The boys were more enthusiastic about the extreme ease of using a computer that the girls, but the support for it as a way of working was generally very positive.

The students were clear that the computers offered two distinct advantages. The first was access to material, and the second the ability to improve the presentation of their work. The presentation skills are not just a matter of word processing but include spell checks and dictionaries, cutting and pasting and using PowerPoint. Desktop Publishing makes students aware of how their work can be set, with added pictures and graphics, different font sizes, and all the techniques of drawing attention to what they are conveying, like bullet points.

This awareness of presenting work goes deeper than adding a gloss to their work. As with some styles of poetry, there is also an awareness that how they create and present their work is also part of what they want to say. In this way, the technique becomes part of the message, just as the text messages and mobile phones create a new kind of communication system and just as "blogging" is pursued as a new art form. Students are therefore learning not only about the presentation of work but also about the additional material they can add from various sources. They also learn about the possibilities of transmission and videotexting.

When all the different uses of the computer are considered, then the skills involved become more than mechanical routine. They can be developed in imaginative ways. This depends essentially on use, on exploring ideas that go beyond what they are being told about them. While one central interest in computing is about the presentation of material, another favourite pastime is playing games. From the school's point of view, the question is whether these games include transferable skills, or whether they merely take up time.

It is often argued that games and simulations have a significant role to play in developing skills, even if the student is unaware that this is happening. Thus the student who is involved in a "shoot 'em up" computer game might be learning about problem solving and logical thinking as well as hand-to-eye coordination. Is the student involved in an adventure simulation or in a game which involves other people, learning about identity and role play, or merely escaping to the land of fantasy? Do the stories that these games solicit stir up the same kinds of interests as Tolkien or Pullman, or are they simply crude manipulations of heroes and villains?

Simulation and adventure games teach skills and cognition when they present challenges. Simulations can be made from real environmental problems, of the kind that fit in to the main traditions of cognitive psychology (Vygotsky 1962). While computers can be an escape, they can also be stimulating. Strategy games like puzzles and "army action" games can develop a sense of tactics and logistics. Role play can involve more than taking a part in a shoot-out, the mowing down of the lurid figures or crashing about in a tank or fast car. It can include the need to understand circumstances and to plan (Papert 1980, Scaife and Wellington 1993, Cox 1994). Skilled use of ICT can mean that students are interpreting results and testing hypotheses (Laurillard 2002).

To what extent are such games and simulations used in school? The students clearly associate home with the place that is the main site of such experiences. Given the cognitive value of such programs, there is no reason that simulations and games should not be part of the curriculum if the curriculum is meant to include skills as well as knowledge. Despite this, just a quarter of the students reported "playing games" at school. While this is an advance on earlier studies when 5% of girls and 10% of boys played games in school (Culley 1986), this is still surprisingly low. The opportunities for playing serious games and for taking part in simulations – from town planning and personal roots, to historical documentation and environmental problems – are many.

The restraint on using the resources of simulations is understandable. The curriculum is overburdened, and there is little time for imaginative exploration. There is "more important" work to be done and exams to be prepared for. Such games seem, in comparison, frivolous and a recreational rather than cognitive enhancement.

There are different types of games, and the students were asked to describe the kinds they took part in within the confines of school. Of that small proportion who had access to games, 17 reported using role-play games. A larger category was sports-based games, which 34 students made use of. Forty-six of them (far more boys than girls), took part in action games and 51 of them in strategy games. Rather more – 66 students – reported playing educational games, although the distinction between those that sound respectable and strategy games, or role-play, is difficult to detect.

All these computer games can test the players' decision-making skills. Action games demand a response to information on the sub-cerebral level, with quick interactions rather than considered thought. Yet all of these play a small part in the experience of school. The curriculum is not geared to such activities, and the facilities are limited. Teachers tend to believe that if pupils play such games in the classroom they will not concentrate on the formal curriculum (Loveless 1995). The times when pupils were allowed to play games were confined to the end of the lesson as rewards if they had finished their work. It was seen as a frivolous activity, rather than an educational tool.

The games that computers offer vary widely. While they tend to be associated with the violent simulations that are reported in the press, they also encapsulate versions of almost any traditional pastime from patience to crosswords and more cerebral challenges. There are also many programs like Encarta that offer a variety of interesting sources of exploration. The activity is nevertheless marginalized as an insult to the mainstream of school. When the small number of students who have played games in school were asked when this took place, just 16 said they had played games during an ICT lesson and 28 of them in other lessons. The rest had played games outside lessons, in the breaks, in the library or in computer clubs. The demarcation line between the uses of computing for pleasure and for work is very clear. While there is a school of thought that computer games themselves teach students about programming, this is part of what takes place outside school (Beynon and Mackay 1993).

The computer clubs in some of the schools were in an ambiguous position. They were to encourage students to enjoy the computers, but there still remained an educational imperative to make them learn. Some teachers were asked not to let students bring in games as advisers thought that this might distract them from the seriousness of computers. Some of the computer clubs were dedicated to students doing homework. Even in these periods, outside lessons, games were frowned upon.

The limitations of facilities in the schools were compounded by attitudes towards them. The restricted access to computers was underlined by restricted use. The association of computers with games and entertainment, with exploration and communication, was confined to the home rather than the school. Students like to go on the Internet and think that they learn from it, but feel such learning is not encouraged in the school.

The demarcation line between school and the world outside is clear. This is not so much to do with access to facilities – computers as well as friends are available in both – as with the attitude towards them. There are many things that are not allowed in school.

> We are not allowed to go on all the websites like games, music and things like that, because they are blocked off, which is something to do with the law. (Girl, year nine)

At school, there is an implication that web sites are illicit and a secret pleasure that has no place in school.

> Yeah, I go to Google and just type it and click on "search" but some websites, like the ring tone one, games, music and sports we cannot go into. In school, they don't like it. They are all blocked off, but at home, you can do whatever you want to do. In school, if you go on these websites you get warnings. And if you do it three or four times you get caught, and your teacher does not put you back on. But at home, I can talk to my friends. I can download to music, save it on my own PC, and I do what I want to do because of my own computer. (Girl, year ten)

For the students there is a clear command not to use the computer as they would at home. The teachers are pictured as keeping an eye open for anyone not strictly concentrating on the set tasks, even if they are gaining access to valuable information. Some teachers will allow students to go on the Internet after they have completed work, but others forbid even this reward.

Students would like to have access to the Internet and are aware of what it can offer, but are aware of the controls of the school.

> You need permission, though, to go on the Internet. Otherwise you are not allowed to do that without a permissions slip. Teachers can see what you're doing, if you are doing any work or not and if we are not doing our work. They don't actually use the Internet. (Girl, year nine)

The most powerful attributes of computers are banned. It is as if the very association with pleasure contrasts too obviously with the ethos of school.

Many students expressed the wish that they could use the Internet more often. They resented all the restrictions placed upon them. They realized that there were many sites that were banned.

> We are not allowed to use it all the time and some of the sites are blocked. (Boy, year nine)

> Some of the websites are banned, like chat room. (Girl, year nine)

One of the results of such restrictions is a commensurate diminution of pleasure. School is serious, and the work undertaken demands a different kind of attitude. The seriousness of the demands of school is made as clear as the consequences of failing to take it seriously.

> We are not allowed to use the Internet in lessons. Like in IT lessons, we just do what the teacher tells us to do. Sometimes I skive the IT lessons as I don't like it much. It's really boring. In school, you are not really allowed to go on the Internet. There are some websites which are blocked, because I like to go on them all the time, so they don't let you go on one. (Boy, year nine)

There is an unself-conscious logic that states that the websites are blocked specifically because he likes to go on them.

The Internet offers all kinds of possibilities, and these are eschewed in school. It is still a means of learning, even if it contrasts with the experience of learning from teachers. ICT lessons have been characterized by their concentration on skills, on the instructions that students carry out. The duty of the students is to adhere to the teacher's wishes and to follow what they say closely and attentively. The Internet might be a source of knowledge, waiting to be used, but the teacher knows exactly what should be learned. To ensure that this is so, they are willing to make it absolutely clear to all what their demands are. The centre of attention is the teacher rather than the learner. Rather than seeking out information, students are required to respond to it.

> They do go over and over it again just to make sure. That and they will ask you questions on the subject, to make us learn it. Sometimes they say the same things over and over again four or more times. But I don't really find it boring. Like if they explain it twice, just in case they don't get it or somebody else don't get it. Just to make sure that I understand that other people understand as well. (Boy, year ten)

He is not being critical. He appreciates the efforts. But the onus is on the teacher to deliver a message, to make sure that all the students take in what he is getting at.

These instructions at the start of a lesson contrast with the idea of a learner seeking help. Sometimes individual attention is just not feasible.

> You put your hand up and he just says, I come in a minute. Then he never does. (Boy, year ten)

In the experience of the school the wishes and commands, as well as attention to the teacher, are vital. There is no freedom of movement or choice of activity.

While it is possible to do little, it is not possible to choose what you want to do. The teacher is the centre.

> Some are all right. You can learn from them, if you concentrate on them, but if you don't get on with them it's not your fault is it? (Girl, year nine)

The concentration is not on the task, but on the teacher.

Whereas it is possible to work at home, to gather material, to balance work with entertainment, the focus in the school is quite different. There is an assumption that students do not come to school with a lot of knowledge. What they do bring is deemed to be irrelevant. What counts is what teachers are supposed to make them learn.

> It is their job to like learning subjects to us. That is up to the teachers if they can make it interesting to us. Like if they are in a nice mood, and they got a nice personality, and they will. If they are boring and horrible then you don't learn that much. Because they don't make it interesting to learn. (Girl, year nine)

Role-playing can involve more than taking a part in the mowing down of lurking figures or racing on the fortunately simulated motorcycle or fast car. It can include the need to understand circumstances and to plan (Scaife and Wellington 1993, Cox 1994). Skilled use of ICT can mean that students are interpreting results and testing hypotheses.

Conclusions

Teachers are in the difficult position of teaching something with which the students are already familiar. The very fact that this is pointed out draws attention to the ways in which schools are made to operate. It is still assumed, in the old fashioned way, that pupils are like empty vessels to be filled with all the knowledge of the National Curriculum.

The contrast between the uses of an informal medium and the formal setting of school is clear. Students are accustomed to both and adapt accordingly. They know the demands of school and submit to them as if they had no choice. This has certain consequences; the students talk about the way they are given instructions, but they are also in the habit of waiting to receive them.

This tension of expectations leads to a certain kind of schizophrenia. The computer contains the best and most varied information, but the source of knowledge remains the teacher. The computer is mediated by the experience of school. Games and simulations are rarely used, and many pleasurable activities are banned.

Even computer clubs demonstrate a suspicious attitude to computers as if they should not be used as a source of pleasure. All those activities that students prefer become marginal. The central focus of school remains intact.

Chapter 9

The Uses of Computers

The contrast between the uses of computers in the school and elsewhere is clear. Given the ubiquity of microprocessing and all its various applications, it is no surprise if all forms of equipment are used without much thought, enjoyed without self-consciousness. Those materials and objects we most take for granted are strange if looked at closely for their own sake, novel if studied deliberately. At school, all the accommodations of use, and the easy pleasures of familiarity, are transformed into something else. The computer becomes a matter of moment. Instead of its being a natural part of everyday life, it becomes part of a different culture, that of knowledge in the service of testing.

The reason that the tensions between the subject of the ICT and its servicing of other subjects are so important is because they demand quite different frames of reference. In school, the tasks are laid down, are imposed and controlled by others. Elsewhere, it is the user, him or her self, who is serviced. The microprocessor is the means through which the individual can be in control, and can exploit its potential.

If we therefore question whether students enjoy using computers, we are unlikely to obtain simple or an ambiguous answers. The more conscious they are of the computer, the more threatened they are likely to be. The more they take what computers offer for granted, the less aware they will be of the pleasure they afford. In the curriculum-dominated school the computer is another part of the whole social ediface of school, something to be learned, an object which is part of the organization of different groups, and another opportunity to be found wanting.

We know that students take the computers seriously and that they appreciate all that they offer. They also realize that computers will remain important in their future lives at work, where it will be central in almost any job they do. At home it is the main source of entertainment. Students are at the same time fully aware of the power of computers as a resource with access to the Internet. As a medium of communication, the computer is paramount. Even if students are unaware of all the potential of globalized interaction, they know all about the ability to interact with large numbers of people, singly, or in groups.

Some of the consequences of such communication systems have not yet been fully understood, such as the ability to pass on offence to large numbers of people, for example the advertising of supposed insults to the Prophet Muhammad in an obscure journal in Denmark which led to the murder of innocents in Pakistan. The more obvious consequences are the friendship sites and the constant chatter of "blogging", where people advertise themselves in revealing detail. However, consequences do not trouble those more accustomed to making use of the available systems. Students accept computers as part of their way of life for entertainment and communications, for presentations as well as for transactions.

In the different types of computer use, are students conscious of deriving pleasure from them? Is this awareness in any way translated into the learning process, let alone the exigencies of school?

The students all derived pleasure from using computers in more than one way. There were certain categories that demonstrated what was most important to them. One of these was using computers for work. We know that the presentation of work was important for them, and that they took seriously all the potential of having access to interesting programs. And yet only 21% of them derived pleasure from this aspect of computers. This was not because it was the least enjoyable activity – that one can take for granted – but because they actively dislike the association of computers with work, despite the potential.

The more popular activities using computers included using e-mails and entering a chat room. In either case, about 50% of the students cited those two contrasting pleasures as something they enjoyed; the private communication on the one hand, and the public exposure on the other. There were two other activities that gave about three-quarters of the students pleasure. One was playing games. The other was using the Internet. Clearly, the Internet can provide all kinds of information, but it can do more. It is a search engine and several students mentioned Google and other sites of that kind. The distinction between pure pleasure and learning was not so fine, although the distinction between pleasure and work remained.

The Internet, and what it can offer, is for students a pleasurable experience. It has become a central medium for communication, not only the exchange of news but finding out what is going on. The provision of chat rooms and blog sites is creating a new form of contact and information that is taken for granted. Even pleasure is taken as read in those circumstances. The ability to keep up chatting, while at home, not only with the daily friends, but with a wider sometimes anonymous circle, is one that is used on a growing scale, replacing some earlier forms of contact. Those students who do not find the uses of the Internet pleasurable include those who do not have access to it.

The National Grid for Learning is based on the assumption that the Internet is a powerful source of information and should be encouraged. This is not a point so easily taken up by schools. They remain suspicious. It is partly because of the fear of students having access to unwarranted sources and a suspicion that they might be breaking laws on privacy (Descry, 1997). They also worry that pupils might be using the opportunity to pursue private satisfactions, that the Internet gives access not only to chat rooms but also to e-mail. While e-mail can be used for academic purposes it is normally associated with private messages, and unlike the old-fashioned letters, these are never completely private. E-mails are not the sole property of the sender or the receiver.

Teachers are aware of the lack of safety surrounding documents, that nothing is ever completely deleted (although it is not difficult to behave as if it were). Their instinctive worry about the uses of the Internet is not, however, to do with arcane matters of confidentiality or access to the various websites, but with the breakdown between the private and the public. In the circumstances of school, this amounts to a tension between the academic and the personal. What the Internet implies is that all people can have access to all kinds of material at any time. This would not be a challenge as such if this were confined to the home, where it is in the hands of the law (Dworkin 2007). The atavistic concern is that such access is an affront to the hegenomy of the school, with its prerogative to maintain control over what is learned, and how. If the school has to be dedicated to following up the demands of policy then there is a realization that they are challenging and being challenged by an alternative world of playing games, of indulgence, of exploration.

Schools see themselves as having a job to do and in a perfect world (as the policy makers assumed) this would mean being completely uncontaminated by the outside world of parents and private interests, of socio-economic circumstances, of alternative ways of thinking. There is therefore instinctive suspicion of the Internet, not so much because of fears of misuse but because of its challenge to the routines and rules of school. It is difficult to have complete control if students have access to such an array of material. At any moment, they might slip away from the task in hand, to explore something that immediately interests them.

At home, such diversions are natural and encouraged. The pleasures that students derive from the computer are not only the availability of PlayStations but also the communicating power of the Internet. This kind of familiarity with the outcomes of computing enhances students' attitudes to ICT in such a way that it should make their approach to computers in school that much easier. The more familiar they are with ICT the better.

At school, the computer is approached once again as a novelty, as if it had not been experienced before. It is at the service of the traditional processes and the standard type of knowledge to be learned, rather than information to be explored. The attitude of students to computers is one thing. Their experience of computers in school is another. Computers in school are dominated not by the Internet, but by word-processing (Buckingham 2001). Students can find the repetitive tasks they are asked to perform very dull (Mumtaz 2000). The computer at school is approached in a different way than anywhere else.

This has consequences. When students were asked how they enjoyed using computers in school, the results were very clear. Only 6% of the students found the school use of computers really pleasurable. Given all the enjoyment that can be derived from ICT at home, this either surprising or an indication that the two experiences are entirely different. Some 19% of the students, while being less enthusiastic, still found using computers in school enjoyable. Computing was seen as different from other lessons, presenting opportunities to work by themselves. There should not be anything threatening about ICT lessons.

The majority of students felt entirely neutral about computers in school. They felt it was not particularly pleasant. It was a task to undergo. ICT can be taken for granted at home, but such an attitude at school is rather different matter. ICT is taken as part of the general school experience. It does not stand out as being a cut above the rest. Its associations with pleasure or with opportunities were played down, the potential mitigated by the usual atmosphere of school. There were also 40% of the students who found the experience of computers in school positively unenjoyable. This was beyond boredom or apathy or indifference. They associated ICT with negativity, with a firm dislike.

For most students the experience of using computers in school is simply part of the routine. It is another lesson. It is not particularly interesting. One could have speculated that the association of computers with pleasure (as well as utility) would prevail even in the different circumstances of school. Even if ICT was not particularly enjoyable, they would still find it interesting, or there would be enough interest to provide a positive response. When students were asked if they found using computers in school interesting, whatever they used it for, almost 60% said they did not.

Again one speculates how computers can fail to be at least interesting, given all the positive attitudes students hold towards their potential. Even if they do not have the equipment at home, they know about the centrality of computers in people's daily lives and take seriously the importance of ICT in their futures. Despite this, a significant proportion did not even find computers interesting.

This overall neutrality to the interest provided by computers was pursued, to explore further the depths of feeling. There were 4% of the students who remained convinced that computers were very interesting and 5% and found them quite interesting. Given that there were three levels of interesting, one fairly mild, this gives an added gloss of indifference or neutrality surrounding the middle point of the scale. Some 30% of the students found that the computers in school were not interesting at all. They were strongly disenchanted. There was no gender difference.

If the overall attitudes were not positive, the question then arose in which lessons these attitudes had been fostered. Did such general indifference arise because of the way that ICT was taught or the way in which it was used? Again, the question aimed to explore the positive attitudes. Students were asked to say in which lesson they found using computers most interesting. It was a matter of making distinctions. The overall context remained, but they were given the chance to pick up those moments where they felt the most positive. This does not imply that there are at least some moments of extreme pleasure, but it is a way of finding out if the negative attitudes that are associated with ICT lessons were mitigated by other experiences. It could be that the creative uses made of computers in other subjects, from history to music, might demonstrate a quite different approach.

Despite what we have learnt about the ICT lessons in themselves, with emphasis on routines and skills, rather than on the creative uses of the Internet, the majority of students found the use of computers was most interesting during ICT lessons. This could be because there were few other choices and they had to pick one, or it could be that they could recall at least moments of passing interest. In this case, there was a slight gender difference, with more girls than boys finding computers interesting during ICT lessons.

The question then was whether the computer came into its own during other lessons. Some 10% found that the moments of interest arose during other subjects. This suggests that the application of computers had not spread very far. This also leaves more than a third of the students who cited being interested outside any kind of lesson. Some 21% said that they found using the computer interesting after the end of the official school day, when all the formal procedures of school were over, and 14% said that they found computers interesting in computer clubs. This suggests, again, the emphasis in the students' minds on computers as standing somewhat distant from the normal school timetable, but there were special periods, official or not, in which computers would be available for them. Rather than a natural part of the methodologies of teaching, the computers were a separate matter. Only after school, or during lunchtimes were computers interesting for some students. For the majority, however, the experience of computers was a quite separate activity, associated with particular moments.

The association of computer use with clearly demarcated ICT lessons is clear. When the students were asked in which periods they found computers least interesting, 60% said that it was when they were used during other lessons. This suggests that at least the majority of the students had the experience of witnessing the use of computers in support of other lessons, and also suggests a lack of real assimilation as it was then that ICT was at its least beguiling. Some students also found that the after-school clubs, and during the computer clubs arranged in the school day, that ICT was the least interesting, as if they had no choice but to go, or were disappointed. Nearly 20% found the computers were least interesting during ICT lessons.

Rather than having to choose the least relished in a generally high standard of attainment, the students made it clear that they lacked any level of interest. Within this general state of dissatisfaction, 60% were unconvinced by the use of computers in other subjects, and the rest were divided between those whose lowest point occurred in ICT lessons and those who did not appreciate the experience of clubs during or after school. This last is a surprise, given that one would have assumed that computers would become enjoyable outside the usual constraints and demands. It might be that the use of computers outside official school hours is a means of delivering the statutory demands about ICT while also fulfilling the orders about the National Curriculum. It is possible to call extra lessons a "club". If these were voluntary, would they then be deemed to be the least interesting?

In the discovery that even clubs can be uninteresting lies the fact that there is still external control over what should be done. Within the parameters of the school, the sense of order prevails into the careful manipulation of what should be learned. Such clubs are not really private. They can be used for homework or finishing uncompleted tasks. They do not provide additional opportunities to access the Internet. They remain a contrast to the experience of home.

Students were not accustomed to having access to computers between lessons; the timetable and the set tasks dominated. There was one student who, exceptionally, said that he could have access to the computers between lessons. He had almost no timetable and this was found a useful means of keeping him occupied. Such an unusual episode points up the more common experience. The pupils were always being controlled. They were not allowed free access to the Internet. They were told what to do and when to do it. This prevailing notion of order and discipline remained true even of the supposedly more relaxed computer clubs.

For some students the opportunity to stay behind after school to work on computers was a chance to do word-processing. There was a general agreement among staff that the quality of students' presentation was enhanced by the application of computers. They felt that the marks were significantly raised by the appearance of the finished product. Students realized that they could use computers for homework, not only in terms of presentation but in terms of materials. An easy shortcut is offered by clicking on a few key words and a certain amount of adaptation or disguise can uncover information of an interesting kind, a different type of "bricolage".

We know where and when the use of computers is interesting and when it is not. The experience remains one that is carefully controlled and monitored and contrasts with the experience at home. That the computer is central to the lives of students is clear. Whether they like it or not, the computers are also central to students' work. While the overall impression might not be that positive, they must still be aware that the computer has potential to help them in all kinds of ways. They were therefore asked to follow the questions of where and when they were using computers and when other computers were interesting with a question that explored the way in which the computer was most interesting in school.

The answers that were given to the "interesting" use of computers in school were varied, but also telling in their focus. By far the largest number, 50%, asserted that using a computer made their work look better. The prowess at presentation, and the realization of what this meant to their marks, was uppermost in many of their minds, supporting this aspect of academic work done on their own time and attention to its appearance. It was a pragmatic use of computers that struck them most.

The next most significant aspect of computing was similar. The students said that the computer help them to work faster. Not only could the computer enhance the presentation, but it could also make them more efficient. Indeed, not only did many students cite doing their work better but a similar number also pointed out that the computer actually helped them do their work. They had begun to rely on it. They had realized its efficiency, and had perceived that it would, ultimately, become irreplaceable. The next most significant answer linked to, and reiterated, the first about the presentation of work. This was concerned with its effects. The students said that the computer helped them get better marks. The pragmatic centrality of the uses of computers was clear. It helped their work, the presentations and their grades.

All this is central to students. Only when the majority of students reinforced the practical support to the work they handed in did they suggest that there were other aspects of computing that are important to them. A quarter of the students pointed out that the computer gave them different information from what they could get elsewhere. They realized it was a rich and convenient source, an alternative to other possibilities like libraries. This was a clear recognition of the power of the computer, but it was not the dominant one. While it is also pragmatic, it suggests a different level of usage.

If the most interesting aspect of computers in school related pragmatically to the ways in which they could help with work, there was one other answer significant in its contrast. Some 12% of the students acknowledged that the computer could help them think differently. This was the only sign of a realization that was something more than pragmatism involved, that the Internet and the associated possibilities, could make a greater difference.

Such a vision of possibilities, of changing a mode of thought, points up a different kind of world. It might or could be part of the school, but suggests something different. The majority of students in their different ways acknowledge the usefulness of computers for their work and its presentation. In itself this was a kind of separation of the uses of computers at home from that of school. They produced their work at home. They prepared it outside school and came to school essentially to hand it in.

The students mostly concentrated on word-processing or writing their work or "tweaking" it. This dominated their outlook, far more than the range of information on CD-ROM, Britannica, Encarta and other software packages. One of the great differences that computers make is giving individuals sedentary access to a range of materials, both in packages and provided by the Internet. Whether it is this that leads to lateral thinking or problem-solving skills is another matter.

Most students did not accept that they thought differently. They acknowledged the computer as a means to an end and the end remained the same kind of school demand. This emphasizes the significance of presentation, and the outcome. The better marks, however, might not simply be due to the way that the finished work looks. It could be that the computer has been a more subtle aid.

> I do find that you get better marks when I use a computer for my work. But I think this is because when doing work on the computer you think about what you're doing more. (In Cuthell 1999, p. 29)

The potential of the computer was clear to all the students. This does not mean that they associated the potential with school. It is as if it were something of greater salience in the outside world than in school. It might be a useful weapon to be wielded by the students in the fight for good grades, but it was not of huge interest in school. In whatever way they were asked, the students did not find the computers of central interest in the circumstances of school. When they had to choose in which lessons and how the computers might be interesting, the answers were also revealing. They demonstrated a pragmatic sense of utility, rather than any excitement.

The distinction between the world of the Internet and that of school was clear. At school students could not be independent, they could not use the Internet or play games or do all those things they would at home. The hegemony of the school remained complete and separate.

The most laconic answers the students gave were around the fact that computers were interesting but not in school. The very fact that they were asked questions about their pleasure or interests associated with school computers made them laugh. They were negative or dismissive of ICT lessons both in terms of their subject matter and the manner in which they were conducted. They did not evince much awareness of teachers' interest or concern. They saw them, instead, driven by targets and outcomes.

When the students were asked to summarize their experience of computers in school they were clear and consistent.

> I find IT boring and all the work we do was boring because it do the same stuff every week. I find it boring, because it's not interesting to learn the same things every week. I don't know why we have to learn the same things again and again. (Boy, year nine)

This demonstrates the way in which computers are used not for access to a range of materials and experiences but as a complex skill that needs to be learned. The syllabus deals with spreadsheets and processing rather than information, with the mechanics of the subject rather the pleasure of its use. To the students these are not very complex skills. Many of them are using them on a daily basis. It is no surprise that the word "boring" keeps recurring.

The students appear to be resigned to a regime of endless repetition and few rewards. This leads not only to the frustration of boredom but the lack of trust in ICT and also what offers.

> You don't really learn much. I'm not really happy about it. I don't think it's good at all. It just annoys you. You really need to get help from other people. (Boy, year nine)

Even the help that is sought remains outside the classroom and, more significantly, beyond the computer, a machine confined to the task in hand, cut off from the very connections that make it powerful.

> You can't just talk to your friends on the computer because it will be boring, but not everything you want to know is on the computer. You have to go to the library and read the books if you want to get all the information. (Boy, year nine)

While one lauds the fact that there are other more useful and reliable sources of information than the Internet, this is a sign of restriction rather than a symbol of old-fashioned values. All students are aware of the limitation of word searches, and the very mixed quality of what is on offer, but that is not what is meant. It is the fact that schools restrict what can be accessed. The same girl spells this out. "The teacher makes it boring".

This is the result of the pressure on teachers to teach to a syllabus, to cram matter into their students. They are not free to unleash the possibilities that computing offers. This means that the routines of school are paramount.

> Because he tells you to do something and if you don't understand it. He doesn't help you. He wastes your time. We do the same things every week, and it is really boring. The work which we are doing is meant to be in year ten, and we're doing it in year nine. (Girl, year nine)

Whatever the possibilities or the merits of the subject it is difficult for students if the traditional habits and familiar associations with school prevail. However liberated the teachers might want to be, they are bound upon the wheel of duty, to reiterate certain routines, to insist on the learning of certain skills. The emphasis on facts is shown in students' awareness of what is appropriate from particular years.

> We don't really do anything that much except looking up video presentation of things and we are not even meant to be doing that in year nine. Its very boring and hard. (Girl, year nine)

The ease and facility of information technology is replaced by demands. Students find such treatment difficult to accept.

> It's just boring. Teacher acts funny, and people start laughing. We are not learning much. (Boy, year nine)

The style of learning imposed by school remains the same and is not adapted to the use of computers. The very resource that could liberate individuals is confined and restricted to particular outcomes and uses. The classroom ethos predominates.

> We're not allowed to use computers in our free time. (Girl, year nine)

The emphasis is on control. Such concern with mastery is not just over facts or even teaching but the style of learning. While a great deal can be learned from peer groups and students enjoy discussions, this is inimicable to the expectations of school.

> It's just boring. Because when you're working with your friends, you can talk about all different stuff and everyone else can give their own opinions, and that

makes it better. When you're working with your friends is more enjoyable and when you are on your own you just get bored. (Boy, year nine)

With the advent of ICT and its access to sources of learning, are schools defending simply an outdated concept of learning? Or are they trying to preserve academic discipline that will otherwise be lost? What is the experience of computers within the whole experience of school?

Conclusions

The tensions between ICT as a subject and its use as a means of support to other subjects is clear, and points up the anomaly that underlines the experience of school. The way in which the computer works is a matter of being used as a means to an end, as an access point rather than something to be studied. And yet, the least popular uses of the computer were when they were a part of other subjects.

Students are accustomed, outside school, to using computers in particular ways. They use it at a variety of levels, sometimes combining several tasks at the same time, while keeping an eye on the news and other events. The screen can be divided into sections so that many activities are available. This is a different way of working.

When computers are experienced in school, they are not associated with pleasure. The generally negative attitudes are pervasive. Anything near school, or associated with school, appears to bring out the same reaction; computer clubs are not found to be exciting. This lack of excitement, of spontaneity or sheer fun, leads students to be pragmatic; the computer at least helps them present their homework in a more efficient way.

Chapter 10
ICT in the Context of School

The contrasts between the experience of using a computer and the general life of the school are clear. Looking at the screen and manipulating the keyboard gives access to an array of information but it is an individual task. Experience of school is a collective one, where groups of different sizes dominate, but it is also an enclosed and narrow world. It is very difficult for schools with their structures and their tasks to accommodate what computers offer. While the emphasis through the National Grid for Learning, and the policy of promoting computer skills makes expectations clear and while the cajoling of policy makers is ardent and even strident, the implications for schools and their functioning have rarely been thought through.

The students are in a difficult position. They understand what they are expected to achieve in school, what the tasks are, how expectations can be met. They realize the importance of conformity, of fulfilling set criteria. Even the teaching of computer skills fits into the accepted norms of the single teacher commanding a selected group, of controlling the tasks that have to be achieved. The alternative experience with the students is quite different, even alien to the ethos of schools, let alone alternative. The potential of the computer lies not in the skills employed but the rewards that are offered as a consequence of these skills; access to games, communication and information.

Students understand that, while schools take computers seriously, they do not celebrate what students themselves find so appealing. Using a computer at home contrasts with the use of computers in school. It is almost as if there were a suspicion of the reality of ICT and the Web, as if such individual manipulation of the media were against the central school policy. This private access to computers is akin to talking to each other, something deemed to get in the way of necessary tasks of the classroom. Students learn a great deal of importance from each other (Harris 1998). This includes attitudes and conduct as well as information, but such conversations are separate from the diurnal routines of school. They belong elsewhere. Group discussions, when they take place, are carefully controlled. There is a syllabus to get through. Any alternative dialogue is taken as disruption.

Comparing the individual users of computers to private conversations highlights the dilemma of the students and schools. There is a shared assumption that, while a free conversation is both longed for and fruitful, the only kind of learning that is countenanced is that of the formality of lessons, of time on-task and the achievement of set outcomes. The statutory orders of the National Curriculum, if not the examinations themselves, make clear exactly what ought to be achieved and what the targets are. Informal learning does not enter into this edifice of controlled outcomes.

Yet it is hard to expunge private thoughts and personal conversations. It is impossible entirely to exclude the outside world, the influence of home and neighbourhood and the free flow of thoughts in the peer group. Similarly, it is impossible to dismiss the personal uses of computers when the machines themselves have invaded the formal spaces of school. The whole experience of school can only be understood if we accept the significance of other influences from the wider world. OFSTED and the policy of inspection likes to think of the school has hermeneutic, as a complete sealed entity, but this research once again demonstrates that this is unrealistic and untrue.

The contrasts in the two approaches to computers are demonstrated in the equivocal attitudes that the students put forward. They realize the significance of computers and their importance to their futures. They appreciate all that is offered not only to their entertainment but to their work. Yet they also find being taught about computing boring. They resent the way that even ICT lessons are imbued with the common expectations of school. Instead of feeling liberated and enlightened by the use of computers in school, they feel inhibited and disgruntled.

The experience of computers in this context can only be understood through students' understanding of schooling as a whole. ICT is simply another part of school and is an experience like all others. While much of the work was carried out at home using computers in a private way, schools were appreciated not just as a necessary locus for handing in work but as a social centre. The attitude of students to schooling can be a surprise in their critical distance, and in those aspects that are not part of official or formal expectations.

> Usually in the first session, we just meet up with everybody and talk with each other to see what ... on Monday, what happened on the weekend, and just see what each of us did and reunite with everybody. We just talk with each other and that's what happens in school. We do get told off, like warnings, but we still continue messing about. That's what really happens. (Boy, year ten)

The one aspect of school that is of significance to all students is meeting friends. When explaining what happens in school, it is that which dominates: the conversations and the sharing of the most significant experiences which take place over the weekend. At school, they "reunite" but while this is pleasurable it is also frowned upon. He only has to mention talk, and he has to add "get told off". The warnings and the "messing about" were considered a central part of school, a constant clash between students and teachers that so easily becomes the norm.

Not every part of school is taken seriously. Not every lesson is approached in the same way. The curriculum might be sacrosanct but the attitudes towards it are not. They vary from enthusiasm to avoidance. The phrase, "if it's a lesson I like I calm down quickly" is telling. There are periods when all are working together to the same end but there are many passages of enforcement. The hidden curriculum of school, the interface between personal attitudes and relationships between students, is actually a dominant one.

> Just messing about with my friends. Sometimes I like to go to lessons. It depends which lesson. But if it's just like ICT, I don't listen to the teacher. (Boy, year ten)

The feeling that there is some kind of incipient antipathy is widespread. There is no collective appreciation of the experience of school. Some aspects and some lessons are liked but there is also a shared expectation of boredom and antipathy. "Messing" with friends is contrasted with listening to teachers. It is noteworthy that what could be interpreted as constructive dialogue is dismissed from the formal point of view of school as "messing".

> Mess about with my friends. I don't listen to teachers, what they say, because they don't listen to what we say. In school you don't learn what you want to learn. (Boy, year ten)

The students keep talking about the deep divide between the formal expectations and the personal pleasures. There is a fissure at the centre, where the pupils assume that the things they do are not appreciated and where teachers are assumed to lack any interest. The sense of a lack of dialogue, confrontation and separateness goes deep. The opportunities that schools afford for such clashes are constant and ubiquitous. The pupils submit without grace to the demands – "It's only a detention. You get it done and it's easy" – and they look forward to all the opportunities to escape from the punitive regime.

> I can't wait for dinner time, just to get out of lessons. (Girl, year ten)

The sense that teachers are imposed on them and are distant is widely shared. Conversations with friends are different from contact with teachers.

> Talk with my friends, mess about with them in the corridor. I just argue with the teachers because they just argue. I don't like it when split up from friends. (Girl year, nine)

School is divided into two contrasting experiences: conflicts with teachers whose job it is to make the students do certain things, and conversations with friends, which are pleasurable and are clearly outside the remit of teaching. That is why the notion of conversation as interactions with peers is spoken of in disparaging terms.

> Just dossing with my friends and just chilling really. (Girl, year nine)

The formal experience of school includes the distinct approach to ICT, like other lessons. Real learning is considered to be a different matter.

> I learn and spend most of my time in school by just like messing around with my friends and playing with them. I don't like ICT lessons. In ICT the work we are doing is just too much and it's boring. (Girl, year nine)

The contrast between the pleasures of being with friends and the boredom of the formal routines is constantly reiterated. From the perspective of ICT this is telling because computers belong to both worlds, that of chat rooms, and that of set lessons. It is not computers that are boring in themselves, but lessons in ICT. Computers are associated with a personal experience of communicating, and this is interpreted as being counter to the ethos of school.

> It's not right that you just shut up all the time. You should be allowed to talk to your mates. (Girl, year nine)

Part of the complaint of lessons, including ICT, is that there is no individual freedom, and no personal opportunities to talk.

> Most of the time in school, mess about with my friends, go to lessons. Some lessons are a bit boring and I'm just getting fed up with them. (Girl, year nine)

The two aspects of school, of socializing with friends and undergoing formal lessons, makes the whole experience far more complex than the assumptions that lie behind the National Curriculum, the league tables and the regime of inspection. From the student's point of view, the saving grace of school lies not in the formal outcomes but in the vivid social life. School is a social rather than intellectual centre.

> I play football and mess around in the grounds. Spend most of my time with my friends, but split up in some lessons. Schools are good way of making friends and meeting more people. My friends are good friends, I get on with them and play football. (Boy, year nine)

The great advantage that school offers is the opportunity to meet other people. While there can be many private contacts at home, and the means of at least talking to a variety of people, it is not the same as the congregation of so many in the classrooms, corridors and assembly halls. While school has a serious purpose, from which students are not allowed (or supposed) to escape, its primary advantage and pleasure is social.

> I enjoy school more than at home because in school you make new friends, and there are usually more friends in school to play with. At home, if you live on a

main road, you can't really play anywhere. But in school, there is a big field. We can always play football. So I like school better than home. (Boy, year ten)

The pleasures of school lie in the informal facilities and personal contacts, rather than in the primary or official purpose. While students enjoy the forbidden fruit of "messing" about with their friends, they do not rate the other experiences of school so highly. They keep talking about boredom and being told off. For some this sense of waste of time is easy to accept and the punishments part of the normal routines. For others the sense of frustration and of helplessness goes deeper.

My experience is not so good. School is a horrible place. Lessons are boring like you think that you are just going to horrible lessons and you just bring your eyes down, you start soaking the lesson and stuff like that. (Boy, year ten)

The main sense is of submission and repression. The realization of boredom has joined the desire for anonymity. There is a strong sense that what school stands for is forcing students to do things whether they want to or not. Some argue that this is a necessary discipline and that those who cower at the repression and those do not readily fit in are at fault, but from the perspective of the students, school is not an enhancing experience.

They can do what they want. They can give you detention if they want. (Girl, year nine)

They are witnesses to unpleasant events.

But when you see people being bullied and stuff, you just don't like it. (Boy, year nine)

The feeling of being marginalized is consistent. Students in year nine and ten talk about teachers being "tight" or the lack of real learning, of wasting time.

The sense that schools are an imposition is, of course, not just the daily experience of being ordered to do things, suppressing conversation, of being disciplined by the routines of time. It is a matter of law, not only that students attend, but that they take schools seriously. They are reminded that there is a purpose.

My experience in school is a bit boring, but you have to go really because it is your future ahead of you. (Boy, year nine)

The problem is that the experience, however necessary, is associated with boredom. The same message is constantly reiterated.

> Sometimes you have to do some boring things. It's not all fun and games. Like when you are in your exams or you have to write essays, things like that. (Boy, year nine)

The school is constantly associated with boredom. For some this is an almost continuous feeling during lessons. For others it is evoked only during some of the lessons that demand the most routine of skills, including writing. For much of the time the lessons are undermined by the purposelessness or by the very narrow sense of purpose attached to them. The insistence on writing, from example, stems not only from creating a quiet classroom and keeping students busy, but from having something to test. Beyond school all writing has a purpose. It attempts to convey ideas, it has to have an audience to address. In school, it is the routines that dominate for their own sake. The dread of copying or "doing it again" explains why the sense of boredom is also so resented.

Routine also affects ICT lessons. There are contrasted with life outside school.

> But teachers make ICT lessons boring. It is a lot more fun at home than working in school and listening to teachers. It is more boring and more tiring in school than at home. (Girl, year nine)

Many of the complaints about school come about because of the contrast between the relationships with peers and those with teachers. The sense of boredom comes about because teachers are perceived as having no time for conversation, but as limiting themselves to instructions. They do the talking. They give the commands. The students are there to listen.

If school is a good place to socialize, this does not mean that all is well. "I like school, but not the teachers" (girl, year nine) is a typical attitude, as if one could separate the two. Many find it easy to symbolize their discontent by blaming the teachers, even if less stringently than the government.

> It's really bad. It's bad, because I don't think teachers have got the right attitude. They got bad attitude. (Girl, year nine)

Those who do best at school know how to fit in, in terms of attendance and grades, and even those who suggest that there are parts of school they enjoy are much more inclined to cite their friends as reasons than the different lessons or the facilities.

School, as a society, presents examples of all kinds of behaviour. On the one hand:

> Here are different races and nationalities who come to school. It's good to socialise, to see your friends and to just have a laugh. (Boy, year nine)

On the other:

> This school is letting itself down and suffering. I feel there is a lot of racism.
> (Girl, year nine)

The term "messing about" can have an edge and while it is seen in terms of the comfort of idle chatter with friends it is also associated with forms of mild bullying and teasing.

> Like in class, some people are dubbing each other, make fun of each other or
> being racist. (Girl, year nine)

The amount of time that students spend in school is significant (Rutter et al. 1979). For much of the year, home life is marginalized, which is why the weekends are special. The opportunity that schools give to socialize is therefore more welcome to the students, if not the teachers. In all this time spent in school, a major portion is spent in lessons, but this does not necessarily mean in work. The students were asked to delineate exactly how they spent each day from the routines of registration to the end of the day. In the six hours or more of attendance students immediately drew attention to the varied patterns.

> And you get like little breaks and in between the school like break time and you
> got dinnertime. Obviously they vary for every year. And after dinner, we have
> tutor time. (Boy year ten)

The students are quick to recognize how much time is taken up in small activities. Unlike the teachers, or the inspectors, they are aware of more happening than the set tasks. They cite moving from classroom to classroom, getting books and packing equipment. There are many inroads into the working day and pupils mention this as a significant routine of school.

> In each lesson, we probably work about half an hour, and the rest of the time, we
> just listen to teacher or talk to our friends. (Boy, year nine)

The students are aware of the realities of the experience, the time spent "tidying up" or waiting for something to happen, in queuing and getting ready. This is quite different from the time spent on the computer or the atmosphere of home for it is a collective sense. They know that the teacher "likes a tidy class" and ICT equipment needs to be stored.

> Roughly, we spend about just more than six hours in school but I think only
> we spend about four and a half hours in lessons and even that's not the time we
> spend working. (Boy, year nine)

When students are asked a simple question about how they spend their time in schools, they reveal their awareness of the collective emptiness of waiting, of routines. They know that a substantial part of the school day is being absorbed in housekeeping and in time wasting, a deliberate and accidental hiatus, time when they could be using computers. The experience of school is not simply that of being taught.

> About four to five hours. In the school we go in lessons, work, talk and just play around and we got break times in between. Sometimes I skive from my ICT lessons. When people say I'm going to toilet, and they go outside and mess about . (Boy, year nine)

The reality appears to be of trying to vary the experience as much as possible, by talking with friends, by spending as much time in more entertaining and less demanding activities. While there is a danger of being caught if avoiding lessons, the chances are that with such a mass of people it is almost impossible for teachers to keep a watch on everyone all the time. Given the sense of opposition, and the resentment of being taught, it is no surprise that students should relish the individual escapades and their personal freedom.

> We don't work all the time. We do talk to each other. Your friends support you a lot, and if I didn't have any friends I wouldn't enjoy it. (Boy, year nine)

In this picture of school, that of conversations and personal interests, as opposed to working and fulfilling set tasks, computers are associated not with pleasure, but with the routines of school. They are absorbed into the official collective order of a formal curriculum. The lessons are standardized.

> School starts at 8.45 and finishes at 3.10. In some lessons I work and in some lessons I don't work. I just mess about. In other words, ICT lessons are dull. We don't work all the time in school. If we do, it gets boring. We lose interest in lessons. (Boy, year nine)

The attitude towards the experience of school borders on contempt. Some lessons are dismissed as irrelevant. Others are found so dull that any distraction is necessary to alleviate the boredom. Although they often get "told off" they persist in "messing about" and "skiving". While this might be deplorable, and ultimately to the students' loss, this is the pervasive atmosphere of school. They feel marginalized and disenfranchised from the main purposes of learning, since the curriculum is not about responding to their needs, but about delivering a quantity of information, the relevance of which escapes the students.

ICT symbolizes this failure of purpose. While a computer is the means of personal exploration at a variety of levels, the source of information and a powerful tool for learning, as well as a source of entertainment and communication, it becomes in school another facet of the curriculum with the emphasis on skills and the implementation that depends entirely on the teacher. In school the learning is imposed to an extent that no longer feels like learning.

If the work of school were fulfilling and interesting we would not find the students describing their experience in such negative terms. They do not highlight academic excitement, but try to give the flavour of the daily routine. What they really do is not what they are supposed to do.

> We do our normal lessons, but I don't know how many hours. About five hours. Talking halfway through, chewing, talking to friends. (Girl, year nine)

This does not mean that all lessons were treated in the same way. There was not only plenty of variation of activity within lessons, but each lesson was also approached in a different way.

> I always do some work but I might do more work in one lesson than another. (Girl, year ten)

> It depends what lesson it is. If you like the lessons I will do some work in them and if I don't like the lesson I do something else. (Girl, year ten)

The difference between the organization of the official curriculum, the delivery of which is the priority, and what is actually learned and experienced is clear. It could be argued that in the way that schools are organized such a gap might be inevitable. It might also be conceded that students might not be capable of constant concentration, but what actually happens is unlike time spent on the computer, whatever the program.

> We have five lessons each day and we, like, an hour of each lesson. And we spend probably 30 minutes working and the other half just doing registration and finding out what the work is going to be about. (Girl, year nine)

This level of realism, reminding us of how schools are organized and how it feels to undergo the routines of the everyday, explains many of the more particular attitudes, to lessons, to subjects and to teachers. Teachers are themselves embedded in the routines, the need to organize and control, to force issues, present instructions and fulfil targets. This puts them in an uncomfortable position.

> I don't like IT, because I don't know what we are doing and I don't like none of the teachers and it's boring. (Girl, year nine)

Teachers are associated with the routines as if it were their fault rather than the role they play.

> Half of the time is missed by not listening to what the teacher is saying. Half of
> the time, if I'm telling the truth I'm messing about with my friends. (Girl, year
> nine)

The formal part of the curriculum is shadowed by all the other activities, whether
the shadows are large or small. From the student's perspective, the experience is
a juggling act between pursuing those things which interest them and conforming
enough to the official requirements to avoid detection. There are several strands
of concern and a number of ambiguities that keep reappearing and which overlap.
One of the constant complaints is simply that of boredom.

> I don't like doing the same things over and over again, and it is the same with
> every lesson. (Boy, year nine)

This boredom is alleviated to some extent by the devious pleasure of talking
to others.

> I talk to my friends. It makes the lesson more interesting. And if you talk to your
> friends, they can help you as well. (Boy, year nine)

The problem with friends is that they are both a constructive help and a source
of distraction. What should be one the most fundamental learning aids is interpreted
as undermining, as if all kinds of things have to be hidden.

> They give warnings, and if I carry on I'll get detentions and all that, but we're
> still doing it, though. In most of the time, I don't get caught. (Boy, year nine)

Communicating with other students, far from being interpreted as a natural
and constructive activity, except in the right circumstances, is placed as an
undermining of all that school stands for. Of course there are times when group
work is encouraged and the motivation of the teacher depends on the attitude to
this.

> If the teacher is nice he will let us choose our own groups. I prefer it this way.
> However, if the teacher isn't nice he put us into groups. (Boy, year nine)

The question is whether the control of the teacher even includes relationships.
"We might not like the people that we have to work with" (boy, year nine) is a
typical complaint, since the students assume that one of the most beneficent aspects
of learning is the support of friends. Far from seeing everything as a competition,
they are grateful for any help they can get.

> My friends in school are very helpful. They help you with a work if you're stuck,
> and if, like, you got a problem or they got any. (Boy, year nine)

Friends are held up as support, but teachers begin to emerge as essential enemies.

> Talking with my friends. I meet my friends there. Most of the time, I argue with my teachers, because I don't get along with my teachers. It's boring, all school's boring. Every kid thinks like that. (Girl, year nine)

The message that the pupils present is clear. The school is associated with boredom and the teachers as unsympathetic. Routines predominate. Under this official organization lie the friendships and the more personal aspects of school from which students also learn. The two experiences overlap in ways which are unexpected.

> If I finish it quite quickly, so teacher just sets me more work. So I like just waste time with my friends in the lessons. (Girl, year nine)

Conclusions

The advent of the computer, its facility, its ubiquity and its penetration of every aspect of life that depends on communication, has made a profound difference to the experience of young people. It has also shown how dated schools are in contrast. Those who predicted massive changes have been disappointed. Schools are the essentially the same as they were 100 years ago.

The whole ethos of computing, with its multiple uses, its individuality, combined with its facility of providing instant communication, runs counter to that of school. When the pupils talk about their experience of school, they contrast the strict regime of silence and conformity to the norm with the pleasure of meeting and talking with their friends.

In the two contrasting worlds of talk and silence, students associate computeers with their friends. Computers are like conversations, giving access to opinions and information, and providing dialogue. Computers are social, since they open a world casual iterative contact. But not in school.

There was a time when there were some challenging new ideas about how schools should function, but not any more. The students convey a sense of suppression, in which the pleasures are secret and informal. In this way even the possibilities of ICT are eroded.

Chapter 11

The Contemporary School Experience

Some fundamental aspects of experience have changed, for most people, over the past 150 years. The history books are full of information about different political systems and changing styles of living. We simply need to be reminded of the evolving landscape of experience since the Industrial Revolution to contemplate how many aspects of life that we take for granted are new. The family household is now filled with conveniences, with washing and cleaning machines, television and telephones. We can not only talk to anyone at any time in any place, but travel easily and freely. All this should have, or must have, an impact on culture, and on the way that people think and conduct themselves.

The effects of change, however, are notoriously difficult to measure. Sometimes an obvious difference, like the ability to travel to other countries, appears to make no personal impact at all. Since the early endeavours of Thomas Cook to enable groups of tourists to travel to exotic and interesting locations, the package holiday has dominated people's lives, but the cultural impact is sometimes difficult to detect. Do the groups who find themselves in the sun in Benidorm or Torremolinos really change the way they understand the different culture when all the signs, the bars, the food and entertainment are still resolutely British? Does the fact that the liquor is cheaper, and perhaps foreign, have any more impact that an encouragement of the habitual vice of drinking too much?

The site of most attention, and the one which has most recently entered people's everyday lives, is that of electronic communication as a result of the development of microprocessors. The technological phenomena are apparent: mobile phones and online shopping, constant news and chat rooms. Yet what are the real impacts of this apparatus on the way people think, let alone behave? One can understand why some conclude that the impact is potentially beneficial, with people freely able to exchange views and information, and to organize themselves into powerful groups. One can also understand why others are concerned by the negative effects of all the free communication on standards, not only on literacy but also on abilities to think (Brabazon 2007).

The question of real cultural change is important in this context, partly because of the realization that there is a whole world of information in media that is beyond institutionally organized control, and partly because of the amount of faith that has been placed in it as having the potential to change the world. The measurement of change, even in small institutions, is itself difficult. Knowing exactly what to assess, what information to look for, let alone probing beneath the obvious, is a complex task. We cannot simply apply the assumptions that shape us and come to conclusions. The future is always dangerous, not just because it is unknowable, but because we can never have the experience to deal with it. We should have the knowledge, through history, but in every spur of the moment decision this knowledge remains unapplied, unless it has gone so deep that it is like an instinct.

Much of the literature on change is about institutions, not so much on how they evolve, but on what managers can do to change them. This is an important distinction, because while it is possible to think of an institution as a complex group of people that has a life and culture and ethos of its own, it is contemporary fashion to concentrate on managerialism, on the manipulation of people and structures in order to develop them. This is one symbol of the rise of what is itself a modern phenomenon: the centrality of an organized institution. Nearly every aspect of people's lives is dominated by ever larger and fewer corporate institutions from governments to supermarkets. It was not always like this. The way mediaeval or even eighteenth-century society was organized was obviously different. One of the aspects of this is the new distinction between the public and private (Elias 1982). This has had a profound effect on notions of childhood (Aries 1962). Public institutions now dominate, from law and order to education. From a world in which people fended for each other as well as themselves, to one where the fending is done for them.

The rise of institutionalized life is demonstrated in the schooling system. Although there were earlier examples of organized academies and foundations for learning open to anyone (hence public schools) the mass education system that we know today is only about 150 years old. As a type of organization, schools have changed as little as the buildings, many of them still inhabited. If one were to go back in time into the middle of the nineteenth century, as is often pointed out, one would witness familiar things (Egan 2002). The ways in which classrooms are organized, the assemblies, the tests, the emphasis on the core curriculum, are all unchanged. More importantly, the purpose behind schooling based on an assembly line of skills, a factory model, is intact. While there might be minor changes, in behaviour or uniform, most of the habits of schooling would be very familiar.

In the age of new communication systems, the fact that schools remain essentially unchanged might seem surprising. There are many commentators who wonder why the same system should perpetuate itself (Elliott 1998, Bowles and Gintis 1976). The fact is that the classroom model with a teacher delivering a set curriculum is at the heart of schooling, however distant this might be from the aspirations and expectations of students. Indeed, the contemporary control over the curriculum and its delivery is even more extreme than it was in the past. The idea of targets and testing, the regime of inspection to make sure that the statutory orders are met, the league tables and the emphasis on particular skills, exemplified in literacy and numeracy hours, all demonstrate a mode of thinking about schooling as distinctly Victorian. It is as if all the research on cognition, children's abilities and learning theory had never been taken into account (Cullingford 2008).

The one thing that is clearly different about schools is the context in which they operate. The policies might still centre on the need for a skilled workforce, in order to gain the upper hand in international competition, and the students themselves might still understand the purpose of schooling as being preparation for employment, but they are also aware of a different world. One aspect of this is the fact that schools no longer have control over knowledge. Information is freely available and unavoidable. Some information is sought but most of it is inadvertent: the news, marketing, the constant chatter of the airwaves. The experience of the world is international. This might not mean that prejudice or tribalism have disappeared, but it does demonstrate that students have far more knowledge on which to base their bias.

Students enter a school on order to attain certain kinds of knowledge. This is a different kind from that experienced at home and on the Internet. School knowledge is controlled through the organization of groups, in a shared collective endeavour to receive the same information at the same time. Individualization comes in the form of testing. The knowledge that is acquired in the home is individual and is taken personally from an array of materials. The testing of this kind of knowledge then comes in the form of collective experience, the peer group, in comparisons and social circumstances.

In these circumstances, how do students view the experience of school? What is the purpose? What part does it play in their lives? So far we have looked essentially the way which ICT is introduced and taught and the contrasts of its uses. The context of school, however, is itself important. For all the changes of technology it remains an extremely important experience (Mortimer et al. 1988, Rutter et al. 1979). The students were asked to say what they thought school was for and how it served its stated objectives. They began to explore some of the general attitudes to school.

Despite the neutrality of the question, focusing on the purpose of school and utility of schooling, centring on the sanctioned and legal requirements, the first instinct of the student was to react negatively. Even in its own terms, educational policy appeared to be found wanting. The constant reiteration of phrases like "boring", "waste of time" and "they don't listen to us" was not confined to the disenfranchised and disillusioned. While readily submitting to the attendance of lessons as well as the pleasure of meeting their friends, the formal purposes of the curriculum offered did not suggest great satisfaction or even belief in the system. The divide that students felt between them and their teachers was a sign not of teacher failures but the state of the system. There was a clear rift between two worlds, one private and shared with friends, and the other imposed, implacable and meaningless.

What, to students, appears to be the purpose of schools?

Friends. Getting along with people. Make new friends. To get an education, get good grades at GCSE. To me that's everything why you come to school. You can socialise with people. You can learn things at the same time as well, and it makes, like your real life, really. You come to school, make friends, get an

> education and education gets you a job and I think that is all you want from life.
> Like friends and education. (Boy, year ten)

The meaning and purpose of school (and of life) is summed up in the two poles of the official line in getting an education and jobs, and the private interpretation of meeting friends. To that extent the purpose behind school is clear, as well as the way in which it is supposed to be achieved.

Once conceding the official purpose of the utility of school, far more stress is placed on the more personal experiences. Indeed, for students who contemplate what they have most usefully learned at school, learning how to get on with people is paramount (Cullingford 2002). That is the essence of school as an institution. It draws people together and controls what takes place collectively. When students said what they had learned, they would cite examples.

> You learn about other people's religions as well and you get to know lots of different people. (Boy, year ten)

Whether this is the official purpose is another matter. There was a strong tendency to respond to the idea of what school is for with an immediate "I don't know", before trying to delve beyond the sense of meaninglessness.

> I don't know really. I come to school because I meet my friends. (Boy, year nine)

This could be a personal purpose but for many students it is the other people rather than the curriculum that give a sense of purpose to learning.

> School is the place to know more people. In school, you meet people you never met before. People from different cultural backgrounds come to school. (Girl, year nine)

The school is a central meeting place and its educative function appears to many students to centre mainly on the people who attend. They are the ones who are to be learned from. Friendship is a pleasure. It is also a central motivation to go to school.

> Make friends. You can learn new things. You can learn from your friends. There is plenty of people, you can make friends with and talk around, make fun of people, argue. (Girl, year nine)

School is associated with seriousness and the contrasts between the demands made by officialdom and the temptation to be self-indulgent are often brought to the fore. The main point of schooling is nearly always recognized but the other aspect is never forgotten.

It is safe and big environment of children, to interact with many people. (Boy, year nine)

It is a balance between different kinds of learning that seems to matter to the students; they do not automatically assume that everything is directly connected to the official curriculum.

It's there learning in theory, because you can read and write. I like it because you get to learn, you get to make new friends, and of course, have fun. (Boy, year nine)

The students' theory of learning is intimately linked by the association of learning with other students, as a social activity, even if it is not part of the intended curriculum. The students have clear views of their own which do not coincide with what is officially prescribed. While students submit to the demands, they see the purpose of schooling in their own way.

to learn, to make friends and just somewhere to go. Is like where you make friends. If you are at home, you don't. You don't really see anyone at home. In school you see lots of people, and you make friends with them. (Girl, year nine)

This is not the official *raison d'être* of school, but it makes a sensible one. The need to meet other people and learn from them is acknowledged. Even if this is inimitable with the proper functions of schooling, it is what keeps the students attending. It has become a kind of routine in their lives, the place where they exchange ideas and make friends, and which in this way gives them something to which they look forward.

But I see people making friends and chatting and stuff. There is more happy stuff. Like if you smile then you see lots of people talking and its great. (Boy, year nine)

The side of school which, by the time they are coming to the end of their compulsory years, remains most important is the social one, the chance to meet others.

Like yesterday a new boy came to school, and we played football, so we made a new friend, stuff like that. It's really enjoyable because you are with them. (Boy, year ten)

The students were being asked not about what gives them most pleasure but what is the purpose of school. They kept drawing attention to friendship, to the possibilities of combining learning with meeting others from whom they could also learn.

> As you grow older and you need friends to help, if you're having a bad time. You need your friends to socialise with them and tell them about your problems. I think. (Boy, year nine)

The sense of the importance of friendship is in contrast with the more official purposes of school, the requirement to pay attention. The students are aware of this disparity.

> School is for learning. It's not supposed to be for messing around with your friends. But that is what everybody does. (Boy, year nine)

While school is not supposed to be concerned with socialization, that is still taken by the students as its real purpose. The personal interpretation remains valid, and appears a mitigating factor to all their other experiences of school.

> You don't really want to go to school and you don't want to learn. When you got friends you're happy in your lessons. (Girl, year nine)

It is taken for granted that school is not meant to be fun. There is a grim reality about the communal sense that people would prefer not to be there and cannot wait to be released. At the same time, there is the saving grace of friendship.

> ... to get an education. If my friends weren't there I probably wouldn't like to go to school. I don't like teachers all the time because they are really horrible. (Girl, year nine)

The students do not spend time wondering about whether teachers like to be there. It is assumed that there are two separate sides in school. One is symbolized as the secret world of the staff room, where the power is deployed. The other is the need for students to put up with this. What school seems to offer, to both camps, is clear.

> Learning and making friends, going to somewhere during the day. It's boring to be in school, like lessons are too long, not enough holidays and teachers are boring. (Girl, year nine)

Learning and making friends are sometimes juxtaposed against each other and sometimes joined. It is, however, clear that the joys of friendship are what makes school worthwhile. Friendships are both a source of pleasure and of learning, and a mitigation against the normal routines of school. If the purpose of schooling is socialization, that is itself a clear indication of what is thought of the rest of the experience.

> My experience is not so good. School is a horrible place. Lessons are boring. But in my experience is bad in school. (Boy, year ten)

The conclusions that students come to are consistently negative.

> It will occasionally get interesting, then you go back to routine. (Boy, year nine)

This is a tired recognition that, even if there are a few good moments, even in the official curriculum, the school is dominated by routine. This is why the word "boredom" is used so consistently. If the work does not suggest a deep purpose then it cannot become enhancing or attractive.

> School is rubbish. It is rubbish. You just don't do anything. You just write. They don't make it interesting like they used to in primary school. (Girl, year nine)

The vehemence about school is usually suppressed, but the exasperation comes about because it seems to be so much a matter of mechanical routines. It is uninteresting doing tasks as if they were designed to keep students quiet, to prevent them from talking to their friends. There is a repressive sense to school that elicits the most negative reactions.

> There's nothing good in school. School is not a nice word. It's horrible. It is horrible when you have to wear a uniform. It just seems a waste of time and money. (Girl, year nine)

The overall impression given of the school is of a resentment at the time spent, the feeling that a lot of time has been stolen from them for no particular purpose. Those things that give pleasure and seem to make sense remain the private ones of friendship and of conversation. In this context ICT should be on the side of personal life; it is also private and a kind of conversation. Its uses in school, however, are wholly dominated by the routines. The experiences of school therefore tend to be associated with negative ones, from those aspects of being bullied or picked on by teachers to the more general sense of boredom. It is as if boredom is so deeply embedded it has itself become almost the purpose of school.

> My experience in school is a bit boring really, but you have got to go really because is your future ahead of you. (Boy year nine)

The contrasts between school and home are often drawn out. From the point of view of the system, home life is an irrelevance. Schools are judged on their internal performance, whatever the social circumstances. They have their tasks to fulfil which are national standards. They are to meet targets and to make sure that all their students learn the necessary skills. Students do not think in this way or have the attitude to school that suggests it can be taken out of context as if a personal life were not relevant. One of the reasons that students talk so much about friendship is because this is what they bring with them into school. In this way, school is a part of their lives, not the other way around.

The virtues and limitations of school are always seen from the awareness of life elsewhere.

> In school your mum can't tell you what to do. You just have fun, like mess about and do your work if you want. (Boy, year nine)

School can even appear an escape from demands. It all depends on how much control the students have over their own time. The problem with school is that conditions are rarely as the students would like them to be.

> Let us listen to music and stuff like that. They don't let you do it. If you can't listen to music, you don't like to work. They don't let you do anything. You just yup on. (Girl, year nine)

This says something about the preferred style of working. Students cannot always understand why there is such an insistence on silence, on preventing people from talking. They are accustomed to doing several things at the same time, talking, listening to music and working. The conditions in which they would like to perform are free and entertaining without pressure or demands. The reasons for going to school, apart from seeing their friends there, is that students have to. They have no choice.

> Government makes me and it's somewhere to go because there's nothing really interesting on TV during the day. (Girl, year nine)

> Some days I don't really enjoy that I have got to go. My parents will be mad if I didn't and I will get done for skiving. I can't do that because I will get told off and suspended. (Boy, year ten)

They might prefer to stay at home but have no choice. They go to school and that is accepted as a necessary passage in their lives, as employment will be afterwards. Yet this does not mean that school is considered a particularly enjoyable experience. There is resentment as well as boredom. The underlying purpose is not clear. All the experience inside lessons is shadowed by the sense of discontent, of having to put up with things.

The question was about the students' understanding of the purpose of school. There was not even one student who talked about pleasure and enlightenment. These were students doing well, the ones committed to success, in ICT and beyond. The impression they gave suggested a dichotomy between the styles of learning that take place elsewhere and the experience they have in school. Thus they submit to what is necessary, and make use of the opportunity to see their friends.

> Because I want to go to college in a few years and to do that I have to go to school, get good grades, and plus my parents make me come to school. Mainly I come to school to learn, that's probably the first point, and the second is probably to just chat and chill with my friends. (Boy, year ten)

Conclusions

These students are not the disenfranchised or the dysfunctional. They might sound disenchanted, but they represent the typical mixture of young people and their attitudes. They are intending to go on with their studies, since they know that any success in the future depends on this. They all accept that they have to be at school, that they might think what they like but they have no choice. They have to make the best of it.

Should we blame the students for this? We cannot blame the teachers who are forced to follow the statutory orders. Are the experiences of students worse than they were in the past or has schooling always been the same? Is the underlying purpose of school that students must learn to suffer, to submit to unpleasant experiences whether they like it or not?

One thing is clear and that is that there is no clear vision of what school is for; the students try to find their own ideas, but there are no hints of a shared sense of excitement and commitment. In this context, the alternative world of communication and the availability of knowledge stands in sharp contrast.

Students stress the social side of school partly as a defensive measure; it mitigates boredom and normlessness. However, their stress on this is also an important insight. They know that the most important learning takes place elsewhere, and in this the computer plays an important part. One sense of importance lies in going through the system, in taking the exams and passing them, but this is not the same as learning.

Chapter 12
The Electronic Age and Schooling

The shared perceptions of the world will always be dominated by certain shortcuts, phrases and words that seem to summarize received wisdom. Is it inevitable as a way of sharing understanding, but every such word or phrase demands examination. The concept of change is one of the cliches of our time, applied by politicians, not so much as an observation as a command. All times are full of change, but the present shared assumption is that the pace of change is fast and demanding, inevitable and something to which people must learn to adapt. This concept implies that people are helpless, that all the developments of technology and commerce are imposed on individuals who have to use them to survive.

This emphasis on change is symptomatic of a particular understanding of the human condition, in which the driving forces are technological and collective rather than personal. The changes are seen in institutions, in communications, in entertainment and globalization, rather than in habits, conduct and understanding. The changes are detected in the ways in which people work, in their uses of mobile phones and i-pods and in their tastes. Yet how deep are the effects of these changes? Do people change their habits of thought or their beliefs? Do they think differently as a result of technological developments?

When surveying books which analyse the contemporary scene we are normally confronted by two alternative approaches. One is to embrace all change and innovation as exciting as well as inevitable, something that gives a new gloss and a new possibility to life. All that is new is good. The other is to concentrate on what is perceived as the lowering of morals, as if all the innovations were lowering standards of conduct and of taste. Both aspects represent the culture of the time. One can see the power of both arguments, as well as all the evidence that supports them. The truth is that both are right.

Let us take globalization as an example. While the term has meant many different things since the expansion of empires, eastern and western, it has become a reality of action in terms of any kind of transaction, in terms of communication or finance. When the recession takes place in one stock exchange, the panic spreads quickly all over the world. International companies balance cheap labour in one place with large profits in another. Communication services, even those dealing with the most local matters, are outsourced all over the world. The interdependence of the planet in many ways is clear, from the sharing of league tables to the distribution of diseases. Never before have people travelled so much, and never before has so much knowledge in terms of pictures and stories being disseminated.

One would like to conclude that such communication is a powerful tool in understanding. If there is so much interdependency there should be greater tolerance and sympathy for other people and their cultures. Yet we have to realize, with the shock of 9/11, that there are new forms of tribalism and antipathy, deliberate parochialism and suspicions within and between societies that are in no way mitigated by knowledge. While awareness can lead to tolerance, it can also have the opposite effect. Many of the measures of comparison, from league tables of universities to the testing of numeracy, are more likely to lead to envy and competition than they are to enlightenment or disseminating the reasons for achievement.

The introduction of new systems of transport and communication has many impacts, but not all are necessarily beneficial. When looking at the microcosm of schools, we need to bear in mind that the actual effects of change are not only complex but that they matter in terms of the individual (Cullingford and Gunn 2005). It is tempting to concentrate on the power and potential of the technology, but it is important to consider the impact on people, on their sense of threat as well as liberation, on a sense of damaged identity as well as their enlightenment.

Technological change has always been greeted by equivocal and contradictory reactions. The eternal questions about human conduct and meaning remain intact but they are also changed in subtle ways. The arguments that the medium itself makes an impact on the habits and thinking of people is undeniable, as in the case of telephones. The question is exactly what difference is made to what people say to each other, how they think and what kind of language they use. There are also underlying questions of depth, and the styles of behaviour.

The Industrial Revolution, from the harnessing of steam, gave rise to the concept of the mass. At first it was the potential of mass production, but it soon lead to the employment of people in repetitive tasks as units in a function that only had meaning as a whole. Thus "mass" was applied to media and to the "masses" meaning people. Mass production meant the repetition of the same task over and over again in mechanical precision. This gave the opportunity to replace ancient crafts, the individual artefact hand-made and to a different sense of value, encapsulated perhaps by Marcel Duchamp's saying of his fountain: "I did not make it: I chose it". In terms of education, mass production had all kinds of effects, from the rise of the reading public to popular entertainment.

We have already noted that the availability of new forms of entertainment, no longer confined to the few, leads towards the natural pursuit of pleasure and of gratification. What is at first envisaged as a source of enlightenment, like television, as well as books, is rapidly used as a means of passing the time. These layers of satisfaction from the demanding to the ephemeral should always overlap, but there is always a danger of a confrontation between the popular and the elite. This is also seen in schools.

The question of whether technology changes the habits of thought returns us to the work of Marshall McLuhan, the first to popularize the notion that the medium itself is the message. That useful catchphrase, "the global village", encapsulates both the possibility of worldwide communication and the potential of parochialism that adheres to it. There are still some telling insights about the effects of Gutenberg's printing press that are worth repeating. McLuhan's assertions are that:

- Societies have always been shaped more by the nature of the media or which men communicate them by the content of the communication.
- The alphabet and print technology fostered and encouraged a fragmenting process, a process of specialism and detachment.
- Electronic technology fosters and encourages unification and involvement.
- Our "age of anxiety" is in great part the result of trying to do today's job with yesterday's tools, with yesterday's concepts.
- Youth instinctively understands the present environment – the electric drama. It lives mythically and in-depth (*The Medium is the Massage* 1967, first pages).

While one can argue with the meaning of many of these concepts, they still capture, 40 years later, that sense of dichotomy between generations and between media. Although there might be no answers there, the questions are worth answering. When we think of the models of schooling and contrast them with access to ICT we can detect the differences between the use of print technology and all it is meant to imply, and the new digital experience. We can also understand the clash of two quite different environments.

Since Marshall McLuhan there have been many others not only fascinated by change but predicting the end of the great age of the book and book learning (Gomez 2007). The hypothesis is that the digital media will dominate, that the post-modern generations will turn to the screen and a computer rather than to print. Those who have been sucking information and entertainment from the Internet are now cutting and pasting and regurgitating it with pictures of themselves and examples of their taste for all to see, shameless and truly global.

The arguments about the end of books is partly because they are so easily replaced by e-books, by digital files on which information is more easily held and disseminated than on the printed page. However, the argument is not only about convenience but habit. It presupposes that the taste for reading itself, for browsing, for libraries, even for systematic study, is being eroded, that the pleasure of what was known as scholarship is replaced by more utilitarian and immediate sensations. Even academics who teach media studies are horrified by the refusal of students to work, as if even in university standards have been destroyed by Google and Wikipedia (Brabazon 2007).

While all media techniques are ephemeral and fashions are short-lived, they do have their effects. In the world of post-modernist art, a passing phase, like distinct periods of pop art, can remain symbolic of the period. The iconography of graffiti, once derided, is now prized and lucrative and trends like painting on spat out chewing gum or making videos of people in peculiar costumes, are taken into the mainstream. This acknowledgement of the new might seem trendy and passing, but it does influence people's perceptions. The kinds of language used in e-mails and text messaging are different from the more considered forms of letter writing. Examples of fawning e-mails from students presented in academic texts suggest a different approach to contact with tutors, with all the boundaries of formality broken down.

One can therefore detect cultural shifts, as in the use of plagiarism, the gathering together of scraps of information from unreliable sources and the assertion of personal rights over truth. The eclectic use of the Internet suggests an indifference to the empirical art of verisimilitude, so that the very ease of access to information diminishes its reliability. In the use of text messages, conducted as a means of doing something clandestinely and ensuring that a text will be conveyed and received at sometime in the near future, has enlivened a new language. For a generation accustomed 2 tlk 2 U @ tms, literacy denotes something rather different. In Japan, for example, the mobile phone has given rise to what are tiny novels, mostly personal confessions of the details of assorted ordinary lives. These are "books" written and published and read on mobile phones, not only a new medium of communication but a new form of storytelling.

The irony is that the short mobile phone "novels" are akin in their form and structure to the demands traditionally made in school and nowhere else, a complete story a couple of pages long on A4 paper. Otherwise there could be no greater difference from the literary canon. The means of communication are different, and this leads to thinking differently about communication. While the school is an actual assembly of people, there is an undercurrent of yearning for a virtual world of private contacts and conversations, of carrying out several tasks at the same time. What McLuhan cites as an electronic "warm" age can be interpreted as multi-tasking, as a refusal to concentrate immediately on one task at a time.

The electronic age can be interpreted as a culture shock (Hofstede 1991). When set up against traditional institutions and established modes of thinking, culture shock is one way of interpreting the student experience of school. There are two distinct modes of expectation coming together. It is, however, too simplistic to say that the two are in conflict. The interchange and the experience is more complex than that. Nevertheless, the demands of a formal curriculum, never appropriate to the ways in which young minds think, are more clearly distinct from the cultural norms the students bring with them. Once the school was assumed to be the source of learning, more trustworthy and more uniform than parents. Now it is clear that the alternative sources of knowledge are ubiquitous, powerful and constantly accessed, from the news to opinions about the news.

To summarize the changes of the time into a simple contrast is tempting, but untrue. The real effects of culture on individuals are more subtle and more profound. When television dominated peoples' concerns, before the development of the microcomputer, the kind of research that surrounded it demonstrated a desire to emerge with simple formulae. The experimental research models were designed to prove one or other of the two hypotheses, either that the vulnerable children would imitate all that was violent and nasty, relishing and copying the many depictions of murder, sadism and aggression, or that the programs on television would be life enhancing, worthy of emulation and even cathartic.

The research followed the fashions of the time. The producers, having spent so much energy and belief in creating good programs, wanted to believe that they were doing a great job in improving the world. The critics, often mistaking correlations for courses, derided such notions and looked for all that was corrupt. When these kinds of assumptions and these models of research were undermined by actually talking to people and listening to what they said, a quite different picture emerged (Cullingford 1984). This was to the distress of those who wanted the medium of television to have big effects, to be the explanation of why the world was as it was, either very much worse or very much better. There is plenty of proof that the levels of effect by the media are far less extreme and much more subtle.

There is always a temptation to attribute all manner of effects to particular media. Television is a good example. There are still the occasional sensational accusations that violent films are the causes of crime. When television was first introduced and the figures demonstrated rising crime there were many examples of mistaking these trends as correlations, as a way of having the satisfaction of finding someone or something to blame. The James Bulger case of the murder of a child by two young boys is a case where it would be so much simpler to point to a video nasty as the cause of such immature violence than to explore the greater complexities of human nature. Such crimes were perpetrated long before the advent of television, but the desire for simplicity nevertheless dictates the plausibility of a definite effect.

With television, there were those who advocated that all its power to do good, to present information, as in nature programs, with a clarity that no other medium can emulate, and there were also those who found it a simple target for deflecting concerns from elsewhere. With ICT those who advocate its potential abound but there is also a counter-argument, although not so virulently expressed as in the case of video "nasties". The computer games that, like a genre of Hollywood movies, try to make death seem meaningless and human beings expendable are occasionally blamed for corrupting the young. Chat rooms are deplored as luring vulnerable, lonely young people into dangerous relationships. The Internet can create, through the public celebration of private anguish, cults like the incidence of suicide in a small Welsh town. The simple distraction of being constantly on the mobile phone, texting or surfing the Internet can be singled out as having a deleterious effect on the mind.

The questions of the effects of processing in all its guises are still left begging and perhaps always will be since people have the resilience and intelligence to use it in any number of different ways, for good or ill. Those who advocate having to learn about its dangers, as well as promise, simply draw attention to the importance of the deeper values of critical scrutiny, the significance of the empirical and the proper application of the mind (Brabazon 2007). The ways in which computers have changed the way people interact with each other and transformed some of the transactions, from shopping to banking, is clear. What is less clear is the effect that such practices have on attitudes and conduct. Although McLuhan would claim that there are profound and exciting changes that should be celebrated, it is harder to present empirical evidence that make sense of the "inventories" or examples.

There are certain parts of life that do not change. Schools are recognizable as being essentially the same as they were a hundred years ago. The way they are organized and the materials they present are much the same. This is despite the advent of the Internet, and despite the investment in the potential of different kinds of learning. Schools in their present form are simply not equipped to deal with the new technology. This is not for want of effort on the part of teachers, but because of the educational policy that dictates a National Curriculum, relies on tests and imposes an inspectorial regime to force compliance. Nothing could be further from the ethos of the individual with a computer then the insistence on teaching the same material in large classes.

While the siren calls about the splendid potential of computers continue unabated, so do the familiar attacks on teachers. Reports keep pointing out the same thing. Becta, the British Communications and Technology Agency, point out the vast amount that is spent on information technology, many, many millions of pounds a year. There are laptops and interactive white boards. At the same time, the agency points out that, despite this, the performance of schools is extremely disappointing. Naturally, it is the teachers who get the blame and the headlines repeatedly call them "technophobes" (e.g. *The Times*, 7 January 2008, p. 22). This is unfair. The fact is that schools as they are constituted and the educational policy that creates them remain unchanged. Instead of embracing the new technology and understanding what it implies, educational policy pursues at least two contradictory aims, the primary importance of knowledge and the dominating importance of skills. In the case of ICT the tension is between the subject and the way it serves others. The clash between the use of computers and experience of school goes deep.

How then should teachers cope with conflicting demands, both from the policies imposed on them and the fundamental clash of cultures between the experience of students and arrangements of school? It is important for them to use ICT as a pedagogical tool, not making ICT itself the sole purpose of the lesson. The advantages of using ICT should be made use of, but this means recognizing the attitude of the students, their prior experience and the latent interest they have in applying a medium they essentially approve of and associate with pleasure to the demands of the curriculum.

ICT should not be isolated as a in a special room, but with modern networks it should proliferate in every classroom so that it is a genuine service. If there can be a link made between the work the students do at home and their working school, so much the better. The development of laptops means that it is possible to engage large numbers of students in a variety of tasks at the same time. The fact that students have access to the kind of resources and information previously only available in universities can also be made use of. The creative use of ICT depends on its being demanding. The play element can be connected to some very interesting material.

The functional use of ICT can be learned by other means than repeating the skills in a mechanical routine. This is, in fact, how students themselves develop their skills at home. They arrive in school often having carried out far more sophisticated tasks than they are then confronted with. As in the case of reading, they have learned the skill because they understand its purpose. The yearning for understanding and satisfaction drives the learning. If a skill is taught for its own sake it is meaningless.

Students have a favourable and familiar attitude to computers. Because they are in command, because they can manipulate various functions on offer, they can explore those matters that are most salient to them. While DVDs can make access to television programs so much more flexible so that what is both relevant and entertaining is available on demand, the computer offers such facilities automatically.

ICT can itself be a motivator for learning. Whilst students can be put off by the extremes of school, an experience which encourages negative attitudes even towards ICT, they nevertheless appreciate it to the extent of taking for granted what computers offer. There is a fundamental shift in emphasis in which students are responsible for their own learning. This might be disapproved of in the face of the control of the curriculum, but it is a real hope for the future of education. The implications of ICT are such that the ways in which schools function are fundamentally challenged.

Conclusions

This is a book about schools. Its subject is information technology and how it is used, but the heart of the findings concerns the state of schools, and how they operate. The students that reported on their experience were in principle interested in computers, and accepted them as intrinsic to their lives and to their futures. Their experience of school, however, was quite different. They found that it was without a clear purpose, bleak, repetitive and unrewarding.

The question is whether the alternative experience of computers outside school makes the students more disillusioned and more disenfranchised. It could be that the contrast between the everyday and exciting uses of computers elsewhere shows up how very out of date schools are. Instead of having instant access to information, students are confronted by facts, instruction sheets and routine tasks. Instead of working at their own pace at a variety of levels, they are put into groups working to the same end. Instead of the pleasures of communication they are made to be silent, submitting to instructions.

This has been a journey from all the hopes expressed about the potential of computers, and the impact they could make on education, to the stark reality of the controlling National Curriculum, the scrutiny of inspection and the implacability of constant tests. The excitement of learning conflicts with the demands of teaching.

This is not the fault of schools. They are supposed to follow the statutory orders and conform. They are presented with conflicting and incoherent policies. Their difficulties are not just due to lack of money, although a workstation, like a laptop, for each student would help, but because of the lack of clarity about what they should be doing. If computer technology were taken seriously, schools would not exist in the way that they do now.

The schools are doing the best they can. They achieve successes in the face of external difficulties and social problems. At the heart of the dilemma is the fact that there is a fundamental conflict between the nature of schooling and the uses of computers. Schools seem to the students to be outmoded. They operate in ways that do not seem to make sense. All the individuality that students relish, the exploratory endeavours and the sharing of information, as well as the searching for new ideas, appears to them to belong to places far away from school.

If computers were to be at the heart of education, schools in their present form would disappear. The question remains if anyone would dare to do more than hope that computers will one day change things, and instead act on the possibilities. The students who were part of this research came from a variety of schools. While there used to be a demarcation line between grammar and secondary modern schools, there are now several levels of distinction, but the curriculum is carefully controlled in all of them. If schools were given far more freedom, and had the courage to go their own way, they could do so much more, but they would still be up against the difference between the individual freedom a computer gives, with access to a huge range of knowledge, and the narrow, slow and pedantic demands of the state curriculum.

It is clear that students operate their computers at a variety of levels. They exemplify the eclectic gathering of different kinds of information and entertainment. This might seem a new and challenging way of working; it might even seem threatening, but it is at least a possibility that a genuinely different and more successful education system could be set up.

The need to learn is as natural as the desire to be entertained. Computers might be just a different mode of communication, making little profound difference to the users, but, with the backing of teachers, they could be so much more. The potential is still there and still waiting to be used, but it depends not on the creation of new programs but on a new way of working, in places unlike the present models of schools.

References

Alexander, R. (2000) *Culture and Pedagogy.* Oxford: Blackwell.

Al-Haile, F. (1994) A comparative study of the use of computer technology in Qatar and British secondary schools. Ph.D. thesis, University of Wales, Swansea.

Al-Qudah, H. (2002) Students and the teaching of Arabic grammar at Jordanian schools. Ph.D. thesis, University of Huddersfield.

Altick, R. (1957) *The English Common Reader.* Chicago, IL: University of Chicago Press.

Aries, P. (1962) *Centuries of Childhood.* New York: Knopf.

Barker, J. (1971) Introducing informatics developments in England and Wales. *Computer Education* vol. 7, p. 9.

Barker, P. and Yeates, H. (1985) *Introducing Computer-Assisted Learning.* London: Prentice-Hall.

Beynon, J. (1992) *Technological Literacy and the Curriculum.* London: Falmer Press.

Beynon, J. and Mackay, H. (1993) Computers into classrooms; more questions than answers. In O'Shea A. and Self, J. (Eds) *Technological Literacy and the Curriculum.* London: Falmer.

Bork, A. (1985) *Personal Computers for Education.* New York: Harper and Row.

Boulter, L. (1989) Teacher opinion on technology. *Studies in Design Education, Craft and Technology* vol. 21, no. 1, pp. 5–12.

Bowles, S. and Gintis, H. (1976) *Schooling in Capitalist America.* London: Routledge and Kegan Paul.

Brabazon, T. (2007) *The University of Google.* Aldershot: Ashgate.

Buckingham, D. (2001) *After the Death of Childhood.* Cambridge: Polity Press.

Butterfield, E. and Nelson, G. (1989) Theory and practice of teaching for transfer. *Educational Communication and Technology Journal* vol. 37, no. 3, pp. 5–38.

Chandler, D. (1984) *Young Learners and Microcomputers.* Milton Keynes: Open University Press.

Chuah, C. (1987) *CAL: Promise, Potential and Performance.* Working Papers. Advisory Unit. Penang. Malaysia.

Cole, T. (1990) *A Strategy for Information Technology in the Classroom.* London: Kent.

Cox, M. (1993) Technology enriched school project: the impact on children's learning. *Computers and Education* vol. 21, no. 1, pp. 41–49.

Cox, M. (1994) Computer simulation and modelling. In *The International Encyclopedia of Education.* London: Elsevier, pp. 985–998.

Criswell, E. (1989) *The Design of Computer Based Instruction*. New York: Macmillan.

Cuban, L. (1986) *Teachers and Machines*. New York: Teachers' College Press.

Culley, L. (1986) *Gender Differences and Computing in Secondary Schools*. Loughborough: University of Technology.

Cullingford, C. (1984) *Children and Television*. Aldershot: Gower.

Cullingford, C. (1992) *Children and Society*. London: Cassell.

Cullingford, C. (1999) *The Causes of Exclusion*. London: Kogan Page.

Cullingford, C. (2002) *The Best Years of their Lives? Pupils' Experiences of School*. London: Kogan Page.

Cullingford, C. (2007) *Childhood: The Inside Story*. Newcastle: Cambridge Scholars' Publications.

Cullingford, C. (2008) *How Pupils Cope with School*. Newcastle: Cambridge Scholars' Publications.

Cullingford, C. and Gunn, S. (2005) *Globalisation, Education and Culture Shock*. Aldershot: Ashgate.

Cuthell, J. (1999) *Virtual Learning*. Aldershot: Ashgate.

Department for Education (1995) *Information Technology in the National Curriculum*. London: HMSO.

Department of Education and Science (1981) *The School Curriculum*. London: HMSO.

Department of Education and Science (1989) *Information Technology from 5 to 16*. Curriculum Matters 15. London: HMSO.

Descry, D. (1997) The Internet and education: some lessons on privacy and pitfalls. *Educational Technology* vol.7, no.3, pp. 48–52.

Downes, T. (1999) Playing with computer technologies in the home. *Education and Information Technologies* vol. 4, pp. 665–679.

Dworkin, R. (2007) *Is Democracy Possible Here?* Princeton, NJ: Princeton University Press.

Educational Technology Review (2002) *International Forum on Educational Technology; Issues and Applications* vol. 2, no. 2.

Edward, R. (2002) *Children, Home and School*. London: Routledge.

Egan, K. (1997) *The Educated Mind*. Chicago, IL: University of Chicago Press.

Egan, K. (2002) *Getting it Wrong from the Beginning*. London: Yale University Press.

Elias, N. (1982) *The History of Manners*. Oxford: Basil Blackwell.

Elliott, J. (1998) *The Curriculum Experiment*. Buckingham: Open University Press.

Evans, C. (1981) *The Micro Millenium*. New York: Washington Square Press.

Franklin, U. (1990) *The Real World of Technology*. Toronto: CBC.

Freedman, T. (1999) *Managing ICT*. London: Hodder and Stoughton.

Galton, M. and Williamson, J. (1995) *Group Work in the Primary School*. London: Routledge.

Garrison, D. (1993) Quality and theory in distance education. In Keegan, D. (Ed.) *Theoretical Principles of Distance Education.* New York: Routledge.

Gbomita, V. (1997) The adoption of microcomputers for instruction: implications for emerging instructional media implementation. *British Journal of Educational Technology* vol. 28, no. 2, pp. 87–101.

Glaser, R., Homme, L. and Evans, J. (1996) An evaluation of textbooks in terms of learning principles. In Plomp, T. and Ely, D. (Eds) *International Encyclopedia of Educational Technology.* London: Pergamon.

Gomez, J. (2007) *Print is Dead: Books in our Digital Age.* London: Palgrave.

Haq, N. (2006) Pupils' views and experience of ICT in secondary schools. Ph.D. thesis, University of Huddersfield.

Harris, R. (1998) *The Nurture Assumption.* London: Bloomsbury.

Hawkridge, D. (1991) *New Information Technology in Education.* London: Croom Helm.

Heath, S.B. (1983) *Ways with Words.* Cambridge: Cambridge University Press.

Heinich, R., Molenda, M. and Russell, J. (1989) *Instructional Media*, 3rd edn. New York: Macmillan.

Hennessy, R. (1993) *Materialist Feminism and the Politics of Discourse.* New York: Routledge.

Himmelweit, H., Oppenheim, A. and Vince, P. (1958) *Television and the Child.* London: Oxford University Press.

Hofstede, G. (1991) *Culture and Organisations.* London: Harper Collins.

Hoggart, R. (1957) *The Uses of Literacy.* London: Chatto and Windus.

Hollingworth, H. and Eastman, S. (1997) Home more high tech than school. *Educational Technology* vol. 37, no.6, pp. 46–51.

Joachim, P. and Wedekind, E. (1987) Computer aided model building and CAL. *Computers and Education* vol. 6, pp. 145–151.

Karen, E., Watkins, M. and Wilson, C. (1998) Return on knowledge assets: rethinking investments. *Educational Technology* vol. 38, no. 4.

Khalid, H. (2000) The effects of new office technology on secretaries' attitudes and training. Ph.D. thesis, University of Huddersfield.

Laurillard, D. (2002) *Rethinking University Teaching.* London: Routledge.

Lodge, J. (1992) *Computer Data Handling in the Primary School.* London: Fulton.

Logan, J. (1988) Pupils' attitudes towards computers and perceptions of the learning environment. Ph.D. thesis, University of Hull.

Loveless, A. (1995) *The Role of Information Technology.* London: Cassell.

Loveless, A. (2002) *ICT, Pedagogy and the Curriculum.* London: Falmer.

McLuhan, M. (1962) The *Gutenberg Galaxy: the Making of Mechanical Man.* Toronto: University of Toronto Press.

McLuhan, M. (1967) *The Medium is the Massage.* London: Penguin.

Monteith, M. (2000) *IT for Learning Enhancement.* Exeter: Intellect Press.

Mortimore, P., Sammons, P., Stoll, L., Lewis, D. and Ecob, R. (1988) *School Matters.* London: Open Books.

Morton, C. (1996) The modern land of Laputa; where computers are used in education. *British Journal of Educational Technology* vol. 28, no. 2, pp. 77–88.

Mumtaz, S. (2000) *Using ICT in Schools.* Warwick: Centre for New Technologies Research.

National Grid for Learning (1997) *Connecting the Learning Society.* London: HMSO.

Papert, S. (1980) *Mindstorms; Childen, Computers and Powerful Ideas.* Brighton: Harvester.

Papert, S. (1993) *The Children's Machine.* London: Harvester Wheatsheaf.

Perkins, V. (2001) A jigsaw classroom technique for undergraduate statistics courses. *Teaching for Psychology* vol. 28, no. 2, pp. 111–113.

Philips, R. and Pearson, A (1997) Cognitive loads and the empowering effects of music composition software. *Journal of Computer Assisted Learning* vol. 13, pp. 74–84.

Plomp, T. and Ely, D. (1996) Instructional technology: contemporary frameworks I. *International Encyclopedia of Educational Technology.* London: Pergamon.

Pye, J. (1989) *Invisible Children.* Oxford: Oxford University Press.

Reglin, S. (1990) CAL effects on mathematics achievement and academic self-concepts. *Journal of Educational Technology* vol. 18, no. 1, pp. 43–48.

Rutter, M., Maugham, B., Mortimore, P. and Ouston, J. (1979) *Fifteen Thousand Hours.* London: Open Books.

Sapsford, A. and Jupp, W. (1996) *Data Collection and Analysis.* London: Sage.

Scaife, J. and Wellington, J. (1993) *Information Technology in Science and Technology Education.* Buckingham: Open University Press.

Schall, P. and Skeele, R. (1995) Creating a home-school partnership for learning; exploiting the home computer. *Educational Forum* vol. 59, no. 3, pp. 244–249.

Schramm, W. (1997) *Big Media; Little Media.* Beverley Hills, CA: Sage.

Schramm, W., Lyle, J. and Parker, E. (1961) *Television in the Lives of our Children.* Stanford, CA: Stanford University Press.

Science Direct (2001) Computers and education. *The Computer in the Home*, pp. 1–18.

Society for Research into Higher Education (1996) Guild for the Society of RHE.

Somekh, B. and Niki, D. (1997) *Using Information Technology Effectively in Teaching and Learning.* London: Routledge.

Squires, D., Grainne, C. and Gabriel, J. (2000) *The Changing Face of Learning Technology.* Cardiff: University of Wales Press.

Sturm, H. (1991) *Fehrnsehdiktate: Die Veraenderung von Gedanken und gefuelen.* Guetersloh Bertelsman.

Thelwell, W. (2008) The student experience of foundation degrees. Doctorate thesis, University of Huddersfield.

Underwood, J. (1994) Predicting computer literacy: how do the technological experiences of school children predict their computer based problem-solving skills? *Journal of Information Technology for Teacher Education* vol. 3, no. 1, pp. 115–126.

Underwood, J. and Underwood, G. (1990) *Computers and Leaning.* Oxford: Basil Blackwell.

Vygotsky, L. (1962) *Thought and Language.* New York: Wiley.

Wellington, J. (1985) *Children, Computers and the Curriculum.* London: Harper & Row.

Wellington, J. (1988) Information technology in education and employment. Ph.D. thesis, Sheffield University.

Westly, M. (1989) *Inventing the Future.* New York: Macuser.

Willis, J., Johnson, D., LaMont, D. and Paul, N. (1983) *Computers, Teaching and Learning.* London: Dilithium Press.

Yacci, M. (2000) Interactivity demystified. *Educational Technology* vol. 16, no. 2, pp. 15–30.

Index

Author Index